WHY WE'RE CATHOLIC

Our Reasons for Faith, Hope, and Love

TRENT HORN

Published by
Catholic Answers, Inc.
2020 Gillespie Way
El Cajon, California 92020
1-888-291-8000 orders
619-387-0042 fax
catholic.com

Printed in the United States of America

Cover design by Devin Schadt
Interior book design by Claudine Mansour Design

978-1-68357-024-0
978-1-68357-025-7 *Kindle*
978-1-68357-026-4 *ePub*

For

St. Theresa Parish

Phoenix, Arizona

Contents

PART 4: SAINTS AND SINNERS

PART 5: MORALITY AND DESTINY

Introduction

Why We Believe . . . Anything

I WAS SITTING in a booth at a restaurant in San Diego waiting for the religious equivalent of a "blind date" to begin.

A few weeks earlier, some Catholic friends of mine asked me to meet with their son while he was home from college. They wanted me to speak to him because he told his parents he wasn't going to church with them anymore because he was now an atheist. They asked me, "Can you help him see he needs to start going back to church? Can you help him get over all this atheist stuff?"

Then their son, who I'll call Vincent, walked through the door. I raised my hand and he did his best to manage a half-smile before he sat down.

"How's it going?" he asked.

"Good, I'm Trent."

"Yeah, I know."

I didn't expect this to go very well and, to be frank, I understood his lack of enthusiasm about having lunch with me. That's why I decided just to be honest with him.

"You think I'm here to talk you into being Catholic again?"

"Sure, it's why my parents kept asking me to see you," he said.

"Look, I don't think there's anything I can say that's going to make you change what you believe. I just think you should believe in something because you think it's true, not just because it's convenient for you. Does that make sense?"

He nodded in agreement.

"How about this. Why don't you just tell me why you're an atheist."

"I know you wrote a book on atheism, so I'm not going to debate you," he shot back.

"I don't feel like debating anybody over a plate of mozzarella sticks," I responded. "I just want to find out what you believe, that's all."

So for the next twenty minutes I asked him questions. What do you mean by the term "atheist"? What are the best arguments for and against God? What are the worst? What do you think are the good and bad things about the Catholic Church?

By the time our entrées arrived we were having a good discussion. I gently challenged some of his atheistic beliefs but, true to my word, it wasn't a debate. It was just two guys having a deep conversation.

As I dipped my quesadilla into some salsa I said to Vincent, "I think I've got a good grasp on why you're an atheist, and I actually like talking to people like you. You've given this issue a lot of thought, and if I'm wrong about atheism I'd want someone like you to show me what I don't understand."

"Thanks," he said.

"But it's a two-way street, Vincent. Be honest. If you were wrong about the Catholic Church, would you want someone like me to show you what you were mistaken about?"

He took a sip of his soda while he thought the question over, and finally said, "Yeah, I'd be open to that."

"Okay, well, I've spent a lot of time asking you questions, so now it's your turn. Why don't you ask me about what Catholics believe and I'll tell you why we believe that stuff. You can take my reasons or leave them, but I think your parents will be happy that we at least talked about them." Vincent agreed and we kept at it for another hour.

As the check came, he said to me, "I appreciate what you said. I'll definitely think about all of it."

"And I'll think about what you said," I replied. "Remember, it's a two-way street."

A COMMON DESIRE

I don't look at people who've left the Catholic Church or who aren't Catholic as potential "customers." They're just people. They have things they love and things they hate. They may differ from me in lots of ways, but they almost certainly have one thing in common with me: they don't want to be ignorant and they do want to be happy. I became Catholic in high school because 1) I thought it was true, and 2) finding answers to my deepest questions about existence and purpose made me happy.

It would be selfish of me to keep to myself the peace and joy I receive from being Catholic, so I share this "good news" with others. My aim in this book is simple: to explain why Catholics believe what they believe. I haven't given *every* explanation I can think of, because most people aren't in a rush to read a book that is so thick it can double as a step stool. Instead, I've presented the reasons that made the biggest impact on me during my conversion to the Catholic faith.

If you are Catholic, this book should give you a great starting point for discussions with your non-Catholic friends and family. If you aren't Catholic, then I hope you will at least be willing to hear me out, like Vincent did. Even if it doesn't convince you, it should help you have more thoughtful conversations with Catholic friends and family because you will better understand their point of view.

Whoever you are, whether you're a believer, a skeptic, or you're just not sure what you believe, I hope at a minimum this book will encourage you to follow an ancient piece of wisdom: "Test everything, retain what is good."[1]

PART 1

TRUTH & GOD

1

Why We Believe in Truth

WHEN SOMEONE WALKS toward you with clenched fists, it's normal to become nervous. When I saw a student approach me in this way at a Texas university, I feared for the worst. Fortunately, he just wanted to beat me up with words.

When my presentation on the subject "Why Be Catholic?" was finished, he came up to me and said, "You are one of the most arrogant people I've ever met. You think you're right and everybody else is wrong." I was surprised by how angry this man was, and as I began to respond to him several students came over to see what was happening.

"You're saying it's arrogant for me to think I'm right about a religious truth and everyone who disagrees with me is wrong?" I replied.

"Yeah!"

"Okay," I continued, "I think a few people here would probably disagree with you about me being arrogant. Are you right and those people who disagree with you are wrong?"

The young man looked confused for a few seconds before asking, "What are you getting at?"

By now the few students watching had turned into a crowd of dozens. I explained what I meant.

"You're right. It is bad to be *arrogant*, but it's not bad to be *accurate*. If we possess the truth about something, then those who disagree with that truth will be wrong. That doesn't make us better than them, it just means we have to be willing to listen to one another so that we can avoid error and find the truth."

"But there is no absolute truth!" he fired back. "Everybody decides what's true for themselves."

The nineteenth-century French novelist Gustave Flaubert once said, "There is no truth. There is only perception." Is this statement true, or is it just Flaubert's perception?

WHAT IS TRUTH?

Here's the problem with saying "there is no absolute truth": this statement is an absolute truth. It claims, "It is true in all times and all places that no statement is true in all times and all places." But that is as contradictory as saying, "I can't speak a word of English." It makes no sense to claim it is *true* that there are no *truths*.

But what is truth? When we say a statement is true, we mean it "corresponds to reality." It describes the way the world really is. Any statement that describes the world contains either a *subjective* truth or an *objective* truth.[2]

A truth is subjective if it is only true for the person who is making the statement. If I say, "Mint chocolate chip ice cream tastes great," I am telling a subjective truth. When people disagree about such truths they usually say, "That's true for you, but not for me." It may be true for *Trent Horn* that ice cream tastes great, but a person who is allergic to ice cream may say that's not true for *him*. This isn't contradictory because subjective truths describe people's *feelings toward the world* rather than *facts about the world*.

GETTING OUR TERMS RIGHT

- **Subjective truth**: Statements that describe opinions and are only true for the person who makes the statement.
- **Objective truth**: Statements that describe reality and are true for all people.

A truth is *objective*, however, when it does not merely describe how a person feels, but describes a fact about reality that is true for everyone. Whether you love or hate ice cream, for example, it is *objectively* true that ice cream begins to melt when left out at room temperature (provided the room isn't an igloo). Objective truths cannot be true only for some people. They are true or false for everyone because they describe reality, and reality is something everyone has to accept, like it or not.

So what does this have to do with religion or with being Catholic?

ICE-CREAM TRUTH OR MEDICINE TRUTH?

Some people think choosing a religion or a church to attend is like choosing a new pair of shoes or a flavor of ice cream. If it tastes good or feels great, it doesn't matter which one you pick. They think religious truths are *subjective*, and so they aren't true for everyone. This means if something feels right to you, it's as good as any other set of beliefs.

That's why it can seem arrogant if someone says his religion is right and everyone should belong to it. That would be like saying everyone should only wear sandals or eat mint chocolate chip ice cream (though I admit it is a delicious afternoon treat). In both cases we would say, "That may be true for you, but it's not true for me."

But religious truths describe basic, important features of reality, which makes them *objective* rather than *subjective*. Claims about religion are more like "medicine truth" than "ice-cream truth."

Imagine if we chose medicine like we chose ice cream. We might say, "Mmmm, this pill tastes like strawberries . . . I'll have three." You could get hurt or killed by doing that. You might also stay sick or get worse because you didn't take the right medicine. In this case, what matters is not the subjective truth of how the medicine tastes, but the objective truth of what it will do to your body.

The same is true when it comes to religion. Even if you don't believe in religion at all, that belief should be grounded in facts about reality and not just feelings toward religion. The bottom line is that we should choose a church or faith not because of how it makes us feel, but because it is objectively true and objectively good for us.

RELIGION, RAJAHS, AND ELEPHANTS

Have you ever heard the story about the three blind men and an elephant? The first blind man touched the elephant's tail and said it was a rope. The second man touched its large ears and said it was a fan. The third blind man touched the animal's massive side and said it was a wall.

Then, a wise king called a rajah told the three men, "An elephant is a large animal. You each have a part of the truth, but all the parts must be put together in order to find the whole truth. So it is with your religions. Each has part of the truth, but you must put them together in order to find the whole truth."

But combining contradictory and false religions no more produces a true religion than combining rope, fans, and a wall produces a true description of an elephant.

This parable also assumes that someone does have all of the truth—the rajah. How do skeptics who deny there is one true religion know whether they are like the rajah and not like one of the blind men? Is it possible some religions contain more truth than others, and God has given one religion the fullness of truth?

But isn't it arrogant for someone like me to say I am a part of the "right religion" and everyone else is wrong? If I had been born in India, wouldn't I be writing a book called *Why We're Hindu* instead of *Why We're Catholic*? Maybe, but if I had been born in ancient China I might have written a book called *Why We Believe the Earth Is Flat*. Being born in a time or place that is far from the truth doesn't disprove the existence of the truth.

When it comes to believing in a religion or any other basic truth about reality (like the shape of the earth), we all think that we're right and that those who disagree with us are wrong. Even people who ignore religion think they're *right* that religion should be ignored. They also think that those people who tell them they should convert are *wrong*. This isn't a sign of arrogance; it's a sign of a genuine desire to find the truth.

A person, or even lots of people, can be kind and loving and at the same time be mistaken about religion. The loving thing to do is not leave someone in ignorance, but to help him find the truth. In fact, some people have to be right when it comes to religious truths, because in many cases there are no other options. For example, either religious people are right and God exists or atheists are right and God does not exist. There is no third option, and both can't be right because that would lead to the contradiction of God existing and not existing at the same time.

As a Catholic I don't claim that every other religion is 100 percent wrong. Starting with the most basic questions about the world (which means they deal with objective truths), I try to see which religion best answers my questions: Is there a God? What can we know about God from reason? Did God ever reveal himself to man? Which religion has the best historical claim to being the recipient of God's revelation? Does that religion still exist today?

More than one religion is capable of correctly answering some of these questions. For example, if there is only one God then Christians, Jews, and Muslims would all be correct. If God became man, however, then only one of these religions would be correct. As we answer these questions, you'll see that while many belief systems truthfully answer some of them, only one religion consistently and correctly answers all of them. If we care about truth, then shouldn't we find out which religion has these answers?

PROPOSING RATHER THAN IMPOSING TRUTH

In a video he posted online, atheist and magician Penn Jillette described how a Christian approached him after one of his shows and gave him a Bible. Instead of being offended, Penn said the Christian was "a good man." If Christians actually believed their faith was true, he continued, then they should always share it with other people. Jillette said, "How much do you have to hate somebody to not proselytize? How much would you have to hate somebody to believe that everlasting life is possible and not tell them that?"[3]

WHY WE BELIEVE: TRUTH

- ✧ It is contradictory to say it is true that there is no truth.
- ✧ Objective truth describes reality and so it is true or false for everyone.
- ✧ Since religion describes reality, its central claims are objective and can be investigated.

2

Why We Believe in Science

As a child I wasn't very interested in religion, but I liked science. When I was ten years old, our school's Young Astronomers Club got to visit the Jet Propulsion Laboratory in California. In one part of the tour, we stood on a catwalk suspended high above a dozen scientists who were preparing the Cassini spacecraft for launch. As I peered over the railing, I thought of what science had given humanity: things like the Internet, airplanes, and modern medicine.

The next year I entered junior high and decided I would only trust what science could prove. But during my conversion to the Catholic faith a few years later, I realized I had put too much faith in science, and not enough faith in nonscientific ways of discovering the truth.

WHAT IS SCIENCE?

During the Middle Ages, science was defined as "the knowledge of things from their causes"[4] (the Latin word *scientia* means "knowledge"). This included knowledge of natural things, like stars and planets, as well as knowledge of supernatural things, like angels or God. But in 1837, William Whewell coined the term "scientist" to refer to someone who seeks systematic, *natural* explanations for observed phenomena.

Under this new definition, scientists could not use God as an explanation for what they observed. Since God exists beyond the observable, natural world, he couldn't be studied with science—but that doesn't mean God does not exist.

A metal detector can't detect diamonds, but that doesn't prove there are no lost gemstones at the beach that may have fallen out of someone's piece of jewelry. Like metal detectors, the "thought tools" we use to investigate the world have limits, and the limit of science is the boundary of the natural world. There may be something beyond that boundary, like God, but we need other tools besides science in order to find out.

Some people think science is the only tool we should use to investigate the world and we shouldn't believe anything that can't be proven scientifically. This attitude is called *scientism,* and it's self-refuting because there is no scientific experiment that proves the only reliable form of knowledge is science. In addition, we believe in many things that can't be proven with science.

If in answer to the question "Is science important?" you say yes, how would you prove that scientifically? There is no experiment or machine that shows science is important. Instead, we use logical reasoning to prove this truth and many others.

For example, science can tell us how the world *is,* but it can't tell us how the world *ought to be*. Science gave us airplanes and medicine, but it also gave us atomic bombs and nerve gas. Science can't show us what is good or evil because it is just a tool that can be used for either good or evil. We need other thought tools, like philosophy and personal experience, in order to understand truths about the world that science cannot discover—including truths related to who or what created the world.

A SCIENTIST REVEALS THE LIMITS OF SCIENCE

In 1960, Sir Peter Medawar won a Nobel Prize for research that made organ and tissue transplants possible. He also wrote a book called *Advice to a Young Scientist,* in which he said the following:

"There is no quicker way for a scientist to bring discredit upon himself and upon his profession than roundly to declare—particularly when no declaration of any kind is called for—that science knows or soon will know the answers to all questions worth asking."[5]

Even though he was not religious, Medawar went on to say that we would have to turn to literature and religion for "suitable answers" to questions like "How did everything begin?" and "What are we all here for?"

IS THE CATHOLIC CHURCH ANTI-SCIENCE?

Far from being against science, the *Catechism of the Catholic Church* (CCC)—an official book of Catholic teachings—praises "scientific studies which have splendidly enriched our knowledge" (CCC 283). For example, Pope St. John Paul II told the Vatican's Pontifical Academy of Sciences that evolution was "more than a hypothesis," and Pope Benedict XVI went even further, saying that there were "many scientific proofs in favor of evolution."[6]

But what about Galileo? Didn't the Church persecute him for teaching that the earth revolves around the sun? Doesn't this show that the Catholic Church opposes scientific discoveries that contradict what is established by faith?

First, the Catholic Church did not condemn the heliocentric or sun-centered view of our solar system. According to the online Stanford Encyclopedia of Philosophy, at this time in history "there was no official Catholic position on the Copernican [heliocentric] system, and it was certainly not a heresy."[7] Many scientists in Galileo's time accepted ancient Greek arguments for a stationary earth, arguments that had not been refuted. Today we can use satellites to prove the earth revolves around the sun, but five hundred years ago the question was far from settled.

In fact, Galileo thought the planets orbited the sun in a perfect circle, whereas they actually have an elliptical orbit. Because of this, Galileo's theory could not account for all the observable movements of the planets, which is one reason Pope Urban VIII urged Galileo to treat his theory as tentative. Unfortunately, Galileo chose to mock the pope in his work *Dialogue Concerning the Two World Systems,* in which a character named Simplicio, which means "simpleton" in English, represented the pope's views. Galileo also claimed that Scripture would have to be reinterpreted in light of his findings, a conclusion that lay outside his area of expertise. Both of these missteps led to his famous trial in 1633.

Contrary to popular belief, Galileo was not tortured, but was found to be "under suspicion of heresy." According to his friend Francesco Niccolini, Galileo was placed under house arrest but was given a servant to attend to him until he died of old age.[8] Pope St. John Paul II later apologized for any injustices committed against Galileo during his trial and reaffirmed the positive relationship between the Church and science.

DOES SCIENCE LEAD TO ATHEISM?

Although some outspoken scientists happen to be atheists, according to the Pew Research Center 51 percent of scientists believe in God or a higher power.[9] It's true that scientists are more likely to identify as atheists, but Elaine Ecklund has shown in her book *Science vs. Religion* that science itself doesn't turn people into atheists; atheists are just more likely to pursue careers in science.

This means that there is nothing about science itself that makes it incompatible with religion. Some of history's greatest contributions to science have come from religious people. This includes Catholic friars like Gregor Mendel, who is called the "Father of Modern Genetics," and priests like Fr. Georges Lemaître, who is called the "Father of the Big Bang Theory."

Because of the ever-changing nature of science, the Catholic Church only teaches on matters related to faith or morals. The Church does not infallibly endorse scientific theories, even though it has long supported science. For example, the medieval Church funded scientists who helped create the modern calendar. Today the Vatican operates a large observatory that secular astronomers use on a regular basis.

According to historian J. L. Heilbron, "The Roman Catholic Church gave more financial and social support to the study of astronomy for over six centuries, from the recovery of ancient learning during the late Middle Ages into the Enlightenment, than any other, and, probably, all other, institutions."[10]

WHAT IS FAITH?

When people say, "Science contradicts faith," they usually define faith as "believing without evidence" or "believing in spite of whatever the evidence may say." Science may contradict that *definition of faith*, but not the traditional understanding of faith.

In the broadest sense, faith is just a kind of trust we have in another person or thing. We might say, for example, "I have faith that John will finish our group project." Even scientists have faith that the laws of nature will operate the same way in all times and places, even though they can't prove the laws of nature will always do this.

For Catholics, faith is "the theological virtue by which we believe in God and believe all that he has said and revealed to us."[11] If God does exist (the evidence for which we will examine shortly), then it is perfectly reasonable for people to trust, or have faith, in God, just as we would have faith or trust in other people. This includes trusting what God has revealed to an individual through something like prayer, or in a public way through things like the Bible or the teachings of the Church.

GETTING OUR TERMS RIGHT

- **Faith (common sense)**: A kind of trust we put in a person or thing based on evidence and experience.
- **Faith (religious sense)**: Trust in God's promise based on evidence and experience of God's revelation.[12]

But doesn't having faith mean you don't have evidence for what you believe? After all, if you had enough evidence you wouldn't need faith. But consider this: according to the United States Parachute Association, 99.99 percent of skydivers survive their jumps. Now, imagine you are wearing a parachute you know has been packed correctly and you step toward the door of the plane. As you look down at the ground two miles beneath your feet and see the tops of clouds passing by, I ask you this: "Are you nervous?"[13]

Probably! Even with so much evidence that you will survive jumping out of an airplane you still need to *trust* that evidence. You still need to make a "leap of faith." This is not a blind leap or belief without evidence. It is a reasonable belief that trusts a conclusion based on the weight of the evidence.

With that in mind, let's examine the evidence for the foundational truth of the Catholic faith: the existence of God.

WHY WE BELIEVE: SCIENCE

✧ Science is one tool we use to discover truths about reality, but it is not our only tool, because it is limited to describing the physical, natural world.

✧ We must use other "thought tools," like logical reasoning, to investigate what may lie beyond the physical, natural world.

✧ Faith does not contradict science because faith is not opposed to evidence. Faith is a trust we have in something and, in a religious sense, it is a trust in God's promises.

3

Why We Believe in a Creator

Once during a debate on the existence of God, my opponent tried to use science to prove we should be atheists.

He said ancient people believed in God because they saw things they couldn't explain, like lightning. But science has now explained the cause of lightning and, eventually, it would explain the entire universe. This means there is no need to invoke God as a cause of anything and, therefore, no good reason to believe God exists.

When it was my turn to speak I asked my opponent if he was open-minded. He said, "Of course," to which I asked, "Okay, then what specific evidence would change your mind and convince you God exists?"

He replied, "If you prayed and an amputated limb grew back, then I'd believe." Remembering his earlier statement, I asked him, "If this ever happened, how would you know God was responsible? Maybe science will discover a natural explanation for why the limb grew back."

He thought about my question and then admitted, "I don't know . . . but I mean, how else could that happen unless God did it?"

Now I knew exactly where I wanted the conversation to

go. I said, "If you're impressed by a limb coming into existence from nothing, then why aren't you even more impressed by a whole universe coming into existence from nothing? If only God could regrow an amputated limb, then wouldn't only God be capable of creating an entire universe from nothing?"

Later in the debate I explained to the audience that my arguments for the existence of God did not rely on gaps in our knowledge being ignorantly filled with the phrase "God did it." Instead, the arguments for the existence of God use *positive* evidence to show the universe as a whole could only have God as its cause.

THE FIRST-CAUSE ARGUMENT

Here's a simple argument for the existence of God.[14]

1. Whatever begins to exist has a cause for its existence.

2. The universe began to exist.

3. Therefore, the universe has a cause for its existence.

Even if this argument works, how do we know the cause of the universe is God?

Since the universe includes all of space and time, the cause of the universe would have to exist beyond space and time, because it created those things. This cause would have to be immaterial, that is, not made of matter, and eternal, not exist in time. Since science only studies forces and objects that exist in space and time, this means that the cause of the universe is not something science can ever locate or study. As we've seen, we need another thought tool besides science (like logical reasoning) in order to study the ultimate cause of reality.

REASON LEADS TO A CREATOR

The cause of the universe made space, so it can't be anything that exists in space.

The cause of the universe made time, so it can't be a force that exists in time.

The cause of all existence would have to be existence itself, or what we call God.

If the cause of the universe created something from nothing, then it must be extremely powerful. In fact, if it could create something from nothing, then there is nothing it could not do, and so it would be "all-powerful." Finally, this cause must be personal and can't be a mindless force because it chose to create a finite universe that is only a few billion years old.

An eternal, immaterial, all-powerful, personal cause is what most people imagine when they hear the word "God." But how do we know the universe began to exist? Maybe the universe has always existed and so didn't need a cause.

EVIDENCE FOR THE BEGINNING

You've probably heard of "the Big Bang," which, contrary to what many people think, was not an explosion *in* space but an expansion *of* space (as well as time, matter, and energy) from nothing.[15] According to renowned Tufts University cosmologist Alexander Vilenkin, "All the evidence we have says that the universe had a beginning."[16]

THE FATHER OF THE BIG BANG

In the early twentieth century, the Belgian priest and physicist Georges Lemaître showed that Einstein's new theory of gravity, called general relativity, would cause an eternal universe to collapse into nothingness.

Since Einstein's theory was sound, this only meant one thing: the universe was not eternal but had a beginning in the past.

Fr. Lemaître and Einstein would often discuss the issue while walking around the campus of Caltech. Einstein was skeptical at first, but in 1933 he proclaimed that Fr. Lemaître's theory of an expanding universe was one of the most "beautiful theories he had ever heard."[17] Fr. Lemaître called his theory "the primeval atom," but another physicist, Fred Hoyle, mocked it with the term "Big Bang."

Hoyle believed that theories of the universe beginning to exist from nothing were "primitive myths" designed to inject religion into science. But the 1965 discovery of cosmic radiation from the Big Bang, in the words of Hoyle, "killed" his eternal, steady-state view of the universe.[18] Fr. Lemaître learned that his theory of a universe with a beginning had been vindicated, three weeks before he died in 1966.

We can also show from reason alone that the past cannot be eternal and so the universe had a beginning.

Suppose your Aunt Mildred owns a flower shop and each day she has to count every flower before the shop opens. What if she has a hundred flowers? Piece of cake. A trillion? It may take a little longer. How about an infinite number of flowers? Well, the shop never opens because Mildred never finishes counting.

The universe is like the flower shop: the "OPEN" sign represents today, and the flowers represent every day in the past. If the past had an infinite number of days (or flowers), and every day has to happen or "be counted" before today can happen, then today will never happen, just as the flower shop will never open. But it is "today," so time moved through every day before today. In order to do that, there could not have been an infinite number of days before today. Instead, there must have been a "first day," or a beginning of time, and thus a beginning of the universe, that needs to be explained.

What about the argument's first premise: Whatever begins to exist has a cause for its existence?

Some people say that even if the universe began to exist at the Big Bang, it could have come from nothing in the same way tiny particles have been observed in laboratories to come from nothing. But those particles do not come into existence from pure nothingness. Instead, they come from a quantum vacuum, or a low-level energy field. As philosopher and physicist David Albert wrote:

> Vacuum states—no less than giraffes or refrigerators or solar systems—are particular arrangements of *elementary physical stuff* . . . none of these poppings—if you look at them aright—amount to anything even remotely in the neighborhood of a creation from nothing.[19]

Virtual particles might come to be from fluctuating quantum fields, but it is impossible for anything (including entire universes) to come into existence from pure nothingness. Instead, the universe must have been created by a cause that exists beyond its boundaries of space and time.

THE DESIGN ARGUMENT

Here's another argument for the existence of God:[20]

1. Our universe contains particular laws of nature that allow intelligent life to exist.

2. These laws are either necessary, were produced by chance, or were designed.

3. They are not necessary nor were they the product of chance.

4. Therefore, the laws of nature are designed.

In the past fifty years, scientists have discovered that even a slight variation in many of the laws of nature would have spelled disaster for life as we know it.

Consider the cosmological constant, which represents the strength of gravity in an empty vacuum of space. Once thought to be zero, this constant is actually fine-tuned to the 122nd power—a decimal point with 121 zeros and a one. This constant, or numerical value in a law of nature, could have been 10^{122} times larger than what is necessary for life to exist. Alexander Vilenkin wrote:

> A tiny deviation from the required power results in a cosmological disaster, such as the fireball collapsing under its own weight or the universe being nearly empty. . . . This is the most notorious and perplexing case of fine-tuning in physics.[21]

To put this into perspective, the odds of getting this law of nature right by chance alone are the same as finding a randomly marked atom somewhere in the universe.

GET SOME PERSPECTIVE

- 10^{50}: The number of atoms in the planet earth.
- 10^{80}: The number of atoms in the universe.

> ✦ **10^{122}: The number of ways the strength of gravity in space could have been different and prevented life from existing.**

Some people say that the universe is not fine-tuned for life because so much of it is hostile to life (such as the vacuum of space). But to say the universe is fine-tuned for life does not mean it is a place where the maximum amount of life will thrive. It only means that out of all the possible universes that could exist, it is much more likely that there would have been no life at all. The fact that our universe does accommodate life, regardless of how much or how little, against such incredible odds, requires an explanation.

So what explains these finely tuned laws of nature?

There's no reason to think the laws of nature must allow life to exist, since we can imagine them being different. We can rule out chance, because the odds of getting the laws of nature right are on par with winning fifty consecutive hands of poker in a row—with royal flushes every time![22] (Or one in 10^{300}, and that's a conservative estimate!)[23]

This leaves design.

Like Alexander Vilenkin, the string theorist Leonard Susskind is a nonreligious scientist. But he says in his article, "Disturbing Implications of the Cosmological Constant," that unless this constant's value was designed, "statistically miraculous events" would be needed for our universe to be life-permitting. He suggests that, in light of this, it is possible that an unknown agent set the early conditions of the universe we observe today.[24]

But how do we know this "creator" is God?

Prior to my conversion to Catholicism I was a deist. I believed there was a generic "creator of the universe." But the more I thought about this "god," the more I realized that the creator must be God with a capital "G." God must be infinite and contain all perfections, including perfect love and goodness. Here's what led me to that conclusion . . .

WHY WE BELIEVE: A CREATOR

- Since the universe had a beginning, and the universe includes all space, time, matter, and energy, the universe must have an immaterial cause that exists beyond space and time.

- Science can only study physical objects in time; this means science can never study or naturally explain the cause of the universe.

- The universe contains elements of design and is finite, which means it must have been created by a personal cause and not a mindless force.

4

Why We Believe in God

IN HIGH SCHOOL I only cared about God when I was in a bind on a math test and figured praying couldn't hurt. But most of the time I didn't think the creator of the universe cared about me. Frankly, I didn't care much about him or "it" either. My attitude began to change, however, one Thursday afternoon in my tenth-grade English class.

My teacher offered to grade one of my papers during lunch after my other classmates left, but a few minutes later a group of students came in with pizza—deliciously greasy, buttered-crust pizza from a local restaurant. It turns out the students were part of a Catholic youth group from a nearby church, and my English teacher was the sponsor of their club. I decided to stick around for the pizza and listen to their conversations about religion.

I attended a few more meetings, and I saw that my concept of God was too small to explain the universe. The people in the club helped me answer this question: "Even if the universe has a creator, how do we know that creator is the all-powerful, all-good God Christians worship?"

THE IDENTITY OF THE CREATOR

One way to establish the creator's identity is to rule out options that don't make sense. For example, some people believe the universe created itself, or that God is the universe. This is called pantheism, which comes from the Greek words for "all" (*pan*) and "God" (*theos*).

But if the universe came into existence from nothing, then it would need a cause outside of itself in order to begin to exist. Saying the universe "created itself" is like saying a person conceived himself or that Mark Zuckerberg got the idea to create Facebook from someone who sent him a Facebook message.

But how do you get from what the creator is not, like the universe itself, to what the creator *is*—in this case, an all-powerful, all-good God? One way is by understanding that there must be an *ultimate explanation* of reality.

Imagine you and a friend see a boxcar moving on a railroad track. You ask your friend, "What's pulling that boxcar," and he replies, "Another boxcar." Satisfied? No, because that raises another question: "What's pulling *that* boxcar?"

Your friend's explanation wasn't ultimate or final because it raised another question. Now, imagine this continues until your friend says, "Look, there's just an infinite number of boxcars each pulling the one before it." This may be an infinite explanation, but it's not an *ultimate* explanation. That's because it raises the question "Why is the train moving at all?"

Boxcars sit still unless something pulls them. It doesn't matter if you connect one, two, or an infinite number of them together, they would all do the same thing: remain in place. The motion of the whole train remains unexplained until another entity is proposed: a railroad car that can move itself *and* pull other cars, or a locomotive.

In the same way, our universe's existence can't be explained by an infinite number of other universes that existed before the Big Bang. That wouldn't explain why there are any universes at all instead of just nothing. Instead, another kind of entity must be proposed: a cause that gives existence to all things but receives existence from no thing. In the thirteenth century, St. Thomas Aquinas defined God as *ipsum esse*, which is Latin for "existence itself."

Asking, "If God created everything then who created God?" is like asking, "If the locomotive is pulling the train, then what is pulling the locomotive?" Not every train car needs to be pulled because some cars (like a locomotive) move themselves and explain the movement of all the other cars. Likewise, not everything needs a cause for its existence because one thing (God) is existence itself and explains the existence of all other things.

If God is unlimited being or existence itself, then that means God is *infinite*. That doesn't mean God has an infinite number of thoughts or that he is extended over an infinitely long distance. Instead, something is infinite if it doesn't have any limits. God is the act of being or existence itself and so nothing limits him or his attributes, which include, among other things:

Oneness: Since God has no limits, it follows that he lacks nothing. If there were more than one God, then both of those beings would limit each other in some way. Neither would be truly infinite and so both would be "gods" (or powerful creatures) rather than "God" (the all-powerful creator). If God is the infinite act of existence itself, then there can only be one God.

Omnipresence: God is not "present" everywhere by being identical to everything in the universe (as in pantheism). God is not dispersed through the universe like an invisible gas. Instead, God is present in the universe by sustaining and affecting every part of it. In short, there is no single place or time that contains God. Rather, all places and all times exist because God is existence itself. God perceives all of existence in one eternal "now," and so he is present in it but not a literal part of it.

IS GOD AS SILLY AS ZEUS?

Beings like Zeus and Thor are gods with a lowercase "g." They came from other gods, can die, are limited in power, ignorant of some things, and are usually immoral. They are not the unlimited, perfect act of being that explains reality, which we call "God."

Even intelligent people who lived when these gods were popular didn't believe in them. In his book *Metaphysics*, the ancient Greek philosopher Aristotle called gods like Zeus "myths." However, he said the one, true God "is a living being, eternal, most good, so that life and duration continuous and eternal belong to God; for this is God."[25]

Omniscience: Since God sustains all of existence, he is all-knowing, meaning that he knows all real and potentially real things. God knows not just everything that is true now, but also every real thing about the past (such as how many steps George Washington took in his lifetime) and every real thing about the future (such as whether you will finish reading this page).

But if God knows what I will do tomorrow, doesn't that mean I'm not free to do anything different? No, because God's knowledge of the future doesn't *determine* the future. God isn't in time like you or I. He exists *beyond* time and sees all of it in one eternal moment. Just as me looking at you in the present doesn't stop you from sitting in a chair, God "looking" at you in the future from his position outside of time doesn't stop you from sitting in a chair or doing anything else at that time either.

Omnipotence: Being omnipotent, or all-powerful, means that God has the power to do anything that is logically possible. God can do anything, but some combinations of words are nonsensical and so they don't even count as "things" for God to do. For God to make a "square circle" or "a rock so heavy he can't lift it," or for him to destroy himself, would involve a logical contradiction. As a result, such things do not fall under the category of "anything that can actually be done," and so they have nothing to do with God's unlimited power.

God can do anything, but some combinations of words are nonsensical and so they don't even count as "things" for God to do.

Omnibenevolence: Think about all the bad things in life: cancer, serial killers, times when the fast-food restaurant messes up your order. What do all these bad things, from the trivial to the terrible, have in common? The answer: they're all missing something good.

Cancer is uncontrolled cell growth, so it lacks organization and health. Serial killers are people who lack empathy and love, which would keep them from committing their crimes. And a cheeseburger without cheese, well, that's just a hamburger. So how does this prove God is all-good?

You or I, or any other creature, will always lack something because we have limits. But God has no limits because he's infinite; therefore he lacks nothing. That doesn't mean every good and evil thing is in God because, as we've seen, evil is just the absence of good. Because evil is a lack of good, and

God lacks nothing, it follows that God must be all-good.

All the perfections we see in the world have their source in God. God doesn't just have love, or beauty, or goodness: God *is* love, God *is* beauty, and God *is* goodness. But if God is all-good and all-powerful, then why is there so much evil and suffering in the world? It is to that important question we turn next.

IS GOD A "HE"?

Catholics refer to God as he, but that doesn't mean they think God is a literal male. The Catholic Church teaches: "By calling God 'Father,' the language of faith indicates two main things: that God is the first origin of everything and transcendent authority; and that he is at the same time goodness and loving care for all his children . . . [God] is neither man nor woman. God is pure spirit in which there is no place for the difference between the sexes. But the respective 'perfections' of man and woman reflect something of the infinite perfection of God."[26]

WHY WE BELIEVE: GOD

- Reality requires an ultimate explanation that does not need to be explained by anything else, or what we could call unlimited "being" or "existence" itself.

- This ultimate explanation, or God, must be infinite. Since this cause lacks nothing, that means it alone contains all knowledge and all power.

- God must be all-good because, although he lacks nothing, evil is just an absence of good.

5

Why We Believe God Conquers Evil

People sometimes ask me, "What's the hardest question you've ever answered about the Catholic faith?" They usually expect the question to be a very technical one, but the toughest questions I get tend to be simple and personal:

> "If God is all good, why did he let my son die in a car accident?"
>
> "If God is all loving, then why do children get cancer?"
>
> "If God is all powerful, then why doesn't he fix what's wrong with the world?"

The problem of evil and suffering is one of the oldest arguments against the existence of God. If God is all-good and all-powerful, then evil should not exist. But evil does exist. Therefore, God must either be weak, evil, or nonexistent.

This argument is very powerful on an emotional level, but

from a logical perspective is doesn't prove that there is no God. In fact, objective good and evil provide evidence *for* the existence of God.

WHAT IS EVIL?

In order to understand how God could allow evil to exist, we have to understand what "evil" is.

Evil is not a thing that God created but an absence of good that God tolerates. Evil is a parasite that can't exist without the good just as rust can't exist without the metal it corrupts. Moral evils like rape or murder, for example, can't exist without the good of people who can freely choose to do right or wrong. Natural evils, such as blindness and disease, can't exist without good things like animals or plants.

Even though God didn't create evil, we can still ask, "Why does God allow evils like murder or blindness to exist?"

Evil is a parasite that feeds off the good.

The short answer is this: it's okay to allow evil to exist if by doing so you bring about more good or prevent a greater evil. Humans allow the evil of car accidents, for example, because the regular use of streets and highways brings about a greater good. We could get rid of car accidents by getting rid of cars, but that solution would be worse than the problem we're trying to solve.

Similarly, God could get rid of moral evils like rape by getting rid of human beings or by taking away their free will, but the world would be a worse place if we were all robots. Our world wouldn't have goods like heroism, compassion, or even love, and humans would become the moral equivalents of programmable appliances.

But what about natural evils like disease or disasters that aren't related to our free will? These evils may help us develop virtues that could not exist if God eliminated every instance of suffering. For example, it's impossible for God to make someone be courageous if he is not in danger. They might also be necessary for us to live in a predictable world where God doesn't intervene every five seconds to protect us from pain.

Finally, as limited and fallible human beings, we are not in a position to say God cannot bring more good from any evil we encounter. Imagine a man who stands one inch away from the *Mona Lisa* and says, "This is a terrible painting! It's just some black splotches!" Of course, the man can't appreciate the beauty and goodness of the whole painting because he is only looking at one tiny part of it. In the same way, if we only look at suffering, we lose sight of the big picture, or how God can use suffering to create a good and beautiful world.

Consider the case of Nick Vujicic, who was born without arms or legs. As a child he was so depressed he tried to drown himself in a bathtub. However, after coming to know God and seeing that his life was not an accident, Nick was transformed. He now travels the world to share how God's love penetrates our deepest suffering. He writes, "Even in the worst situations that seem beyond our capacities, God knows how much our hearts can bear. I hold on to the belief that our life here is temporary, as we are being prepared for eternity."[27]

THE HEART OF THE PROBLEM

For a person who is suffering, I understand why this answer may not be satisfying. "I don't care!" she says. "If God loved me he'd take away this pain in my life. He wouldn't let so many bad things happen to people!"

That's a normal response to horrendous suffering, and that's why I agree with my friend and colleague Jimmy Akin, who watched his wife die of cancer shortly after they were married. He says, "God doesn't always give us reasons to explain our suffering, but he does give us ways to help us *endure* it." One thing that helps me endure suffering is the realization that evil doesn't make sense if there is no God.

A lot of people say evil is just "bad things" or "stuff that hurts," but those definitions don't work. Having a cavity filled or being punished for a crime you committed hurt, but they aren't evil. In fact, these are examples of *good* medicine or *good* law enforcement. On the other hand, there can be instances of evil that don't cause pain. A man who fantasizes about raping children but never acts out his fantasies doesn't cause pain, but obviously the man has evil thoughts, not good ones.

Here's a better definition: *Evil is what we experience when things are not the way they are supposed to be.*

Rape, murder, cancer, and other bad things are evil because they distort the way the world should be. Sex should be an act of love, not an act of violence. Cells should grow into body parts, not tumors. If evil refers to the way things are not supposed to be, then good must refer to the way things *are* supposed to be. But if things are supposed to be a certain way, then that means there is both a cosmic plan and a cosmic planner—a planner that many people call God.

AN ATHEIST ADMITS: MORALITY PROVES GOD EXISTS

The atheist philosopher J.L. Mackie wrote, "Moral properties constitute so odd a cluster of properties and relations that they are most unlikely to have arisen in the ordinary course of events without an all-powerful god to create them."[28]

Mackie believed in atheism so strongly that he denied the

existence of objective moral truths, even though they seem real to most people. Perhaps we should accept that morality is real and that it comes from an all-powerful God who is goodness itself.

MEANT FOR MORE

Not only is the universe supposed to be a certain way, you and I are supposed to be a certain way. When society embraces evils like genocide or slavery, the heroes are people who say it's better to do what's right than to accept what's popular. Martin Luther King Jr. even said, "A just law is a man-made code that squares with the moral law or the law of God."[29]

On the other hand, when we do something wrong, even if no one finds out about it, we feel guilty. We feel as if we've failed to live up to a standard of who we were meant to be. Most of us have told someone after we've hurt them, "I'm so sorry, that's not who I am." The reason we feel this way is because God gave us his moral law and wrote it on our hearts in the form of a conscience.[30] The Bible even teaches that people who don't personally know God still know him through their conscience (Rom. 2:14–16).

God gave us the moral law not so that we would feel guilty, but so that we could be truly happy. Imagine how wonderful life would be if no one lied, stole, held grudges, or used another person. Deep down we know we were made to be this kind of person, and suffering in this life can even help us achieve that goal. My favorite verse in the Bible puts it this way:

> Accept whatever is brought upon you, and in changes that humble you be patient. For gold is tested in the fire, and acceptable men in the furnace of humiliation. Trust in him

[God], and he will help you; make your ways straight, and hope in him (Sir. 2:4-6).

GOD'S LOVE AMID NAZI HORROR

One of the inmates at the Nazi concentration camp Auschwitz was a priest named Maximilian Kolbe. After a prisoner was thought to have escaped, the guards selected ten men to die in a starvation bunker in order to teach the remaining prisoners a lesson. The guards began to drag away a man named Franciszek, who dug his heels into the mud on the ground as he cried out, "My poor wife! My poor children!" At that moment, Fr. Kolbe stepped forward and said, "I am a Catholic priest. Let me take his place. I am old. He has a wife and children."[31]

The guards allowed Fr. Kolbe to take Franciszek's place, and over the next two weeks he comforted the other men who had been sentenced to die. Whenever the guards looked into his cell, Fr. Kolbe was either standing or kneeling in prayer. After all the other prisoners had died, the guards did not wait for Fr. Kolbe to starve to death. They instead injected his left arm with carbolic acid and later cremated his remains.

Was this an example of evil that proves God does not exist?

The fact that what the Nazis did was objectively wrong proves there is a universal standard for morality that comes from a universal source of goodness, or God. Morality can't just be a survival mechanism that humans developed through the process of evolution, because some people feel compelled to do things that don't help our survival, like giving their life for a stranger. If we are all made in God's image, however, then that explains our desire to fight and even die for the dignity of someone else. In fact, Franciszek survived his time at Auschwitz and spent the rest of his life publicly speaking about Fr. Kolbe's heroism.

What gave Fr. Kolbe the strength to face such tremendous evil and suffering? As a priest, he devoted his life to imitating Jesus Christ, and Jesus was willing to do anything to save humanity from its sins, including dying a painful and humiliating death on a cross. Because Jesus is the divine Son of God, he was able to offer an infinite, perfect sacrifice of love that made up for the sins of the whole world. For those who believe in Jesus, this sacrifice means death is not the end of life, but rather the beginning of a new life with God in heaven. As he prepared for his execution, I wouldn't be surprised if Fr. Kolbe thought of this verse from the Bible: "O death, where is thy victory? O death, where is thy sting?" (1 Cor. 15:55).

The problem of evil is not God's problem—it's ours.

If there is a perfect, objective standard of goodness, then whenever we choose evil we fall short of that standard. But the moral standards are not like the impersonal rules of mathematics. Morality is about people choosing between good and evil, so the perfect standard of morality must come from a perfect person, or God. This means that whenever we choose evil we separate ourselves from God, who is the Good itself.

Thankfully, by rising from the dead, Jesus showed that anyone who trusts in him would also share in his resurrection to eternal life. God will give everyone who follows Jesus the gift of grace, or the free offer of God's divine life. God's grace equips us to die to ourselves and, if necessary, to die for others.

But how do we know Jesus is God? How do we know he rose from the dead? What if those stories about Jesus are just stories? We have examined philosophical evidence for the existence of God, but now we must examine historical evidence that shows this God revealed himself to the world in the person of Jesus Christ.

WHY WE BELIEVE: GOD CONQUERS EVIL

- Evil is an absence of good.
- A good being can allow evil to exist if he uses that evil to bring about greater goods.
- Objective good and evil only make sense if there is an objective moral law that comes from a perfect lawgiver, or God.

PART 2

JESUS & the BIBLE

6

Why We Believe in Jesus

MANY PEOPLE BELIEVE that there is a God, or at least a "higher power" that created the universe. What they don't believe is that they need to be religious in order to understand God. They ask, "Why should I be a part of a religion like Christianity with all of its rules and hypocrisy? I'd rather be spiritual instead of religious."

SPIRITUAL VERSUS RELIGIOUS

First, it's not bad to be spiritual. A spiritual person knows there's more to reality than physical matter. He may even thank God for the beautiful world he created. But just as most people would love to meet their favorite artist, a truly spiritual person would want to know the artist who created the entire universe. This process of coming to know God and responding to his revelation is the essence of religion.

WHAT DOES THE BIBLE SAY ABOUT RELIGION?

"If any one thinks he is religious, and does not bridle his tongue but deceives his heart, this man's religion is vain. Religion that

is pure and undefiled before God and the Father is this: to visit orphans and widows in their affliction, and to keep oneself unstained from the world" (James 1:26-27).

Hypocrisy, violence, and "long lists of rules" aren't good reasons to reject organized religion, or any organized human activity. Imagine someone who said, "I don't believe in organized sports. Sports leagues are filled with cheaters and the fans are obnoxious jerks. Some of them even cause violence when they riot after games. And there are so many pointless rules! I can be athletic on my own without playing or even watching organized sports."[32]

You can see how this compares to critiques of organized religion.

Just as it would be unfair to say all athletes are cheaters or all sports fans are jerks, it's unfair to smear all Christians as hypocrites. The same is true when it comes to claims of religious violence, like the idea that "religion is responsible for most wars." Sports rioters don't speak for all sports fans and violent religious people don't speak for all the faithful. Most wars aren't fought over religion but for non-religious reasons, such as securing land or natural resources.

What about religion's supposedly pointless rules?

First, every culture has expectations for behavior that, if you wrote them all down, would be a rather long list of rules. Say "please" and "thank you," put away your phone at dinner, take off your shoes when you come into the house, don't dive into the shallow end of the pool, and so on. The NFL's official rulebook is more than 300 pages long—and that's just for one game! Since God loves us, and life is more complicated than table manners or football, we shouldn't be surprised that God's revelation would include a fair number of principles to help us be happy and spiritually healthy.

But how do we know these principles really come from God and weren't just invented by human beings? How do we know which revelation or which religious rules to follow? We can find out by turning our focus to the most important person in all of human history.

THE JESUS QUESTION

When I was deciding whether or not I should be a Christian, I made sure to read about as many other religions as I could. At first it was overwhelming to compare the teachings of faiths like Islam, Hinduism, and Buddhism to Christianity, but then I noticed they all had one thing I could compare: a teaching about Jesus Christ.

NON-BIBLICAL EVIDENCE FOR JESUS

The first-century Jewish historian Josephus said Jesus was a wise man who Pontius Pilate condemned to the cross.[33] In the early second century, the Roman historian Tacitus said Christians received their name from "Christus," who "was put to death by Pontius Pilate, procurator of Judea in the reign of Tiberius."[34] Bart Ehrman, an agnostic scholar who is a leading expert on the Bible, wrote, "The view that Jesus existed is held by virtually every expert on the planet."[35]

Almost every major world religion has a teaching about the identity of Jesus. Jews say Jesus was a human teacher, Muslims say he was a prophet, and Hindus and Buddhists say Jesus was an "enlightened man." They all say basically the same thing: Jesus was a great man, but he's not God. If it turned out that Jesus was God, however, then even though these religions have some good teachings, I knew they couldn't be God's revelation. How could they if they failed to teach about the incredible moment when God became man in the person of Jesus Christ?

Isn't it amazing that even the name *Jesus Christ* can cause tension and discomfort? Some people say it's because that name reminds people of negative experiences they had at church or of violent Christian history. But the words "Christianity" or "Catholic Church" don't cause the same anxiety. I would argue that this name stirs strong feelings in people because the name itself has power. And the name of Jesus has power because the person who bears that name is God in human flesh and has infinite power.

WHAT'S IN A NAME?

- **Jesus**: From the Hebrew *Yeshua*, which means "God saves."
- **Christ**: From the Greek *Christos*, a title that means "anointed one" and has the general meaning of "savior."

Why should we believe such an incredible claim? Here are three reasons:

1. Jesus believed he was God, and we can trust him. Jesus saw himself as more than a human prophet or teacher. For example, Buddha said, "Be ye lamps unto yourselves . . . hold fast to the truth as a refuge,"[36] whereas Jesus said, "I am the light of the world" (John 8:12). Jesus also said, "I am the way, and the truth, and the life; no one comes to the Father, but by me" (John 14:6).

Another clue to Jesus' divine identity is that Jesus acted like God. For example, he forgave sins, which is something that only God has the authority to do (Mark 2:5-7). In John 20:28, Jesus' disciple Thomas addressed him as "My Lord and my God." Jesus did not correct Thomas, because what Thomas said was true.

BIBLICAL EVIDENCE FOR THE DIVINITY OF CHRIST

- Jesus is called God (John 1:1, Titus 2:13, Col. 2:9).
- Jesus acts like God (Mark 2:5–7, Luke 22:29, John 8:58–59).
- Jesus is honored like God (John 20:28, Phil. 2:5–11, Heb. 1:6–8).

In the Hebrew Bible, the name of God was considered so sacred it couldn't be pronounced. Even today many Jews spell the name "God" with a hyphen ("G-d") in order not to disrespect the name. But in John 8:58, Jesus used that sacred, unpronounceable name of God for himself.

He said that "before Abraham was, I am," implying that he eternally existed as God before Abraham, who lived thousands of years earlier. This act infuriated the Jewish leaders and motivated them to kill Jesus for blasphemy. But it wasn't blasphemous for Jesus to use God's name because he is God.

At this point someone might say, "I'll grant that Jesus wasn't a *liar* (since he was a good teacher), and he wasn't a *lunatic* (since he was a wise teacher), but maybe he was a *legend*. How do we know Jesus really said he was God? What if someone added that to the Bible in order to cover up a story about a merely human Jesus?"

This brings us to our next reason.

2. We can trust the New Testament documents.

There currently exist more than 5,500 copies of Greek New Testament manuscripts. There are also 15,000 copies written in other languages like Latin, Coptic, and Syriac. The first complete copy of the New Testament can be dated to within

300 years of the original documents.[37] Now, compare this to one of the most famous examples of ancient Greek literature: Homer's *Iliad*. It was written in the eighth century B.C. and, although a few fragments of the *Iliad* can be dated to within 500 years of Homer, the oldest complete copy was written in the tenth century A.D., or 1,800 years later!

Because there were so many copies of the New Testament in the ancient world (including thousands more that didn't survive to the present day), no single person or group could have gathered them all up and changed the story of Jesus. Also, unlike the biographies of people like Alexander the Great or Buddha, which were written centuries after those figures died, the Bible's descriptions of Jesus were written within a few decades of his death either by eyewitnesses or people who knew the eyewitnesses to Jesus' ministry.[38]

The biblical scholar F.F. Bruce put it bluntly: "There is no body of ancient literature in the world which enjoys such a wealth of good textual attestation as the New Testament."[39]

3. The first Christians worshipped Jesus as God.

The earliest Christian writings show that they believed Jesus was the "image of the invisible God" (Col. 1:15), in whom the fullness of deity dwells bodily (Col. 2:8-9). Jesus had the "form of God" and a name to which every knee shall bend (Phil. 2:5-11). The Bible even calls Jesus "our great God and savior" (Titus 2:13).

When a second-century Roman governor named Pliny the Younger asked Christians to worship the gods of Rome, they refused. In a letter explaining this behavior to the Roman emperor, Pliny said that Christians "were in the habit of meeting on a certain fixed day before it was light, when they sang in alternate verse a hymn to Christ as to a god, and bound themselves to a solemn oath."

Remember also that the first Christians were converts from Judaism. For more than 1,000 years the Jewish people made themselves distinct from their pagan neighbors by refusing to worship an animal or a man as God. The Jews of Jesus' time would never have believed Jesus was God unless his miracles, including his resurrection from the dead, proved it.

Since Jesus did prove he was God, we can trust him when he says, "I am the resurrection and the life; he who believes in me, though he die, yet shall he live, and whoever lives and believes in me shall never die. Do you believe this?" (John 11:25-26).

THE LITTLE FLOWER OF JESUS

In 1887, Henri Panzini was found guilty of a brutal triple murder in Paris. Fourteen-year-old Thérèse Martin, the youngest daughter of a devout Catholic family, heard he was unrepentant, and prayed night and day that he would not go to hell. She then received news that as Panzini's head was placed under the guillotine, he reached out for a crucifix a priest was holding and kissed it three times. She wrote in her autobiography about God's answer to her prayer:

"What an unmistakably sweet response! After this unique grace my desire to save souls grows each day . . . the thirst of my poor little soul increased and it was this ardent thirst he was giving me as the most delightful drink of his love."[40]

Thérèse desperately wanted to become a nun, but her local bishop refused because she was so young. A few months after Panzini's execution, Thérèse met with Pope Leo XIII, and her request was granted. She called herself "the little flower of Jesus" because she thought of herself not as a magnificent rose, but as a simple wildflower blooming where God planted her.

Even though she died of tuberculosis at the age of twenty-four, her autobiography has inspired countless people to follow Jesus and glorify him in any circumstance, no matter how humble. Ironically, the simple wisdom of the Little Flower has had such a profound impact that, in 1997, Thérèse was declared a Doctor of the Church. Of the approximately 10,000 saints the Catholic Church recognizes, only thirty-six have been granted this title.

WHY WE BELIEVE: JESUS

- ✧ If God exists and revealed himself to man, then we should not be surprised he has given us a way to respond to him, or what some call "organized religion."

- ✧ Jesus claimed to be God, and he is too good to be a liar and too wise to be a lunatic.

- ✧ Textual evidence shows that the Bible can be trusted and that Jesus' claims to divinity were not a later legend that was added to the Bible.

7

Why We Believe in the Resurrection

THE BIBLE SAYS that if Jesus did not rise from the dead, then the Christian faith is worthless (1 Cor. 15:17). However, if Jesus did rise from the dead, then we know Jesus can keep his promise to give everyone who follows him eternal life (1 John 2:25). But how can we know that Jesus really rose from the dead and that the Bible's description of this miracle wasn't just a story someone made up?

One way is by showing that the Resurrection is the only explanation for the events surrounding Jesus' death, events that almost everyone, including skeptics, agrees are historical. Even scholars who don't think the Bible is the word of God admit it is not completely made up. For example, skeptical scholar John Dominic Crossan denies that Jesus rose from the dead, but he says, "That he was crucified is as sure as anything historical can ever be."[41]

Similarly, the atheist New Testament scholar Gerd Ludemann said, "It may be taken as historically certain that Peter and the disciples had experiences after Jesus' death in which

Jesus appeared to them as the risen Christ."[42] Lüdemann doesn't think Jesus actually rose from the dead, but that the apostles experienced a hallucination instead. He does think, however, the apostles *thought* they saw the risen Jesus, and this fact of history needs to be explained.

As we examine the various theories put forward to explain these facts, you will see that only one theory explains: 1) Jesus' death by Crucifixion; 2) his empty tomb; 3) the post-Crucifixion appearances to the disciples; and 4) the disciples' willingness to die for their faith: the theory that Jesus actually rose from the dead.

THE SWOON THEORY

One way to explain these facts would be to posit that Jesus never really died. Maybe he just passed out on the cross and woke up in a tomb. Jesus then met up with the disciples who mistakenly thought he'd risen from the dead. But even if Jesus somehow survived the Crucifixion, the apostles would never have thought he'd miraculously risen from the dead. Upon seeing his bloody, mutilated body, they would have thought Jesus had *cheated* death, not beaten it, and quickly gotten him medical treatment.

Besides, there is almost no chance Jesus could have survived being crucified. In 1986, the American Medical Association published a paper that analyzed ancient records of the Crucifixion.[43] It came to the conclusion that it would have been nearly impossible for Jesus to survive the intense flogging that ripped his skin apart as well as the asphyxiation brought on by being crucified.

THE TRASH THEORY

How do we know Jesus wasn't just thrown into an anonymous grave and was forgotten until the disciples imagined they saw him alive again? We'll discuss the theory that the disciples hallucinated in a moment, but let's first consider the idea that Jesus received a dishonorable burial and his body was abandoned in a common grave for criminals.

Deuteronomy 21:22-23 prohibited the Jewish people from leaving a criminal hanging on a tree, so Jesus would have to have been buried immediately after he died on the cross. In fact, the only skeleton archaeologists have from a first-century crucifixion victim was found in a tomb, and not a random plot in a criminal's graveyard.[44] Jesus' burial in a tomb is also described in all four Gospels and corroborated in Paul's first letter to the Corinthians.

The Gospels say Joseph of Arimathea, a member of the council that condemned Jesus to death, buried him (though John 3:1-2 tells us Joseph was a disciple of Jesus, but in secret, out of fear of the other Jewish leaders). If the Gospel writers had invented the story of Jesus being buried in a tomb, they would have given their leader an honorable burial at the hands of his friends and family.

This means we have good historical evidence that after the Crucifixion Jesus' body was placed in an identifiable tomb and simply didn't vanish in a common graveyard.

THE HALLUCINATION THEORY

Most historians agree the disciples thought they saw the risen Jesus. The story of Jesus appearing to them was not a legend that developed centuries later, but was recorded by the apostle Paul (1 Cor. 15:3-7). It is almost universally recognized among historians that Paul existed, we have the letters he wrote, and Paul knew the people who claimed to have seen the risen Jesus (Gal. 1:18–19). But could those experiences have just been hallucinations brought on by the terrible grief these men endured after Jesus was executed?

First, it is individuals, not groups, who almost always experience hallucinations. Multiple biblical authors confirm that groups of Jesus' disciples claimed to see him after his death (Luke 24:36–49, 1 Cor. 15:5–6). As psychologist Gary Collins writes, "By their very nature only one person can see a given hallucination at a time. They certainly aren't something which can be seen by a group of people."[45]

Second, the theory that Jesus' depressed disciples hallucinated his resurrection doesn't explain why enemies of the Church came to believe in the Resurrection. The most famous example would be St. Paul, who was a Jewish leader who persecuted the Church until an encounter with the risen Christ moved him to join the "Jewish heresy" he had been persecuting. The best explanation for such a sudden conversion is that Jesus really did appear to Paul, just as he had appeared to his other disciples after his resurrection.

AN ATHEIST ADMITS: THE EVIDENCE IS OVERWHELMING

Antony Flew was at one time one of the most famous atheists in the Western world. His essay "Theology and Falsification" is one of the most widely printed essays in the history of twentieth-century philosophy. That is why it is remarkable that even he admitted in a debate with a Christian that "the evidence for the Resurrection is better than for claimed miracles in any other religion. It's outstandingly different in quality and quantity."[46]

For example, the Qu'ran does not record Muhammad performing miracles, and the earliest sources about Buddha say he refused to perform miracles.[47] Both men are described as performing miracles only in legends written centuries after their deaths. This stands in sharp contrast to the accounts of Christ's resurrection that we find in the Bible. Unlike the stories of other ancient wonder-workers, these Christian accounts were written decades (not centuries) after the events they describe and are preserved in multiple sources.

THE EMPTY TOMB

Soon after a close friend of mine died a few years ago I had an incredibly vivid dream that she was alive. If I had experienced her presence when I was awake, I would have checked her grave and, if it was empty, then I would know I hadn't been hallucinating. This brings us to the simplest argument against the hallucination theory: at any time the apostles could have visited Jesus' tomb to see if there was a body in it, which would prove that the Jesus they thought they saw was just a hallucination.

We've already seen that it is historically certain Jesus was buried in a locatable tomb. The Gospels tell us that on the Sunday after the Resurrection a group of women discovered the tomb was empty. But why should we believe Jesus' tomb was empty and that the authors of the Gospels didn't make this up? There are actually three reasons and they can be summarized in the acronym JET.[48]

First, the disciples preached the empty tomb in the city of Jerusalem. If the tomb were not empty, enemies of the early Church could easily have taken the body out of the tomb and proven Jesus did not rise from the dead.

Second, the earliest enemies of the Church agreed that Jesus' tomb was empty. Matthew's Gospel says the Jewish leaders of his day (about forty to fifty years after the Crucifixion) believed Jesus' body was stolen from the tomb (Matt. 28:11-15). The second-century Christian writer St. Justin Martyr also says that the Jews of his time believed Jesus' body was stolen.[49] I'll explain in a moment why that theory fails, but notice that these critics didn't say that the disciples merely hallucinated—they had to explain why Jesus' tomb was empty.

Finally, the Gospels include the testimony of women discovering the tomb. In Jesus' time a woman's testimony was considered to be as reliable as that of a child or a criminal. A collection of ancient Jewish wisdom called the Talmud says, "The words of the Torah should be burned rather than entrusted to women."[50] The Jewish historian Josephus said that a woman's "levity and boldness" made her testimony unreliable.[51] If the Gospel authors had invented the story about Jesus' tomb being found empty, they would have used trustworthy characters like Peter or John. The embarrassing detail about women discovering the empty tomb was included in the story simply because that's what really happened.

WAS JESUS' TOMB REALLY EMPTY?

J—Apostles preached in **Jerusalem** where an empty tomb could be disproved.
E—**Enemies** of the faith agree the tomb was empty.
T—The embarrassing **testimony** of women is unlikely to have been made up.

THE FRAUD THEORY

Is it possible the disciples stole Jesus' body and then told people their Messiah had risen from the dead? It's not impossible, but this theory seems extremely unlikely. That's because there's no evidence of any crack in the conspiracy—no record of a single Christian admitting after the fact that it was all a hoax. Moreover, fraud is normally committed for personal gain; the only thing the disciples had to gain from their fraud was persecution and death. Since people don't knowingly die for a lie, we can be confident Jesus' disciples really believed in the Resurrection they preached to others.[52]

Of course, people throughout history have died for many things they thought were true. Muslim suicide bombers die for the Islamic faith because they believe God will reward them in heaven, but their sincerity does not prove Islam is correct. The key difference, however, is that Muslim suicide bombers are not in a position to know if Islam is false (they never interacted with the Muslim prophet Muhammad, who lived centuries before them). The apostles, on the other hand, were in a position to know whether Christianity was false by examining Jesus' tomb and seeing if his body was still there.

There is no chance they were all deceived or that they all chose to die painful deaths in order to deceive others. What's more likely is that Jesus' resurrection really happened and gave them the courage to share this good news in the face of persecution. They knew that even if they were to die through Christ they would live forever. We, too, can have eternal life if we trust in God's promises and choose to be baptized into the Resurrection of Jesus Christ (Rom. 6:3-5).

"I'M READY TO BE A CHRISTIAN"

I remember staying up one night in high school watching debates on the Internet between Christians and atheists. One question kept bothering me: How did it all start? Christianity didn't begin with one person having visions of God that no one else could confirm. It began with the public proclamation that a man had been raised from the dead. It was accompanied by historical evidence, like the empty tomb that proved this was not a hoax or a hallucination. That night I realized Jesus was really alive and he was the God "out there" I had vaguely thought about for so many years. I then bowed my head, opened up my palms, and prayed, "Jesus, if you're real, help me believe. I'm ready to be a Christian."

WHY WE BELIEVE: THE RESURRECTION

- ✧ Even skeptics admit that Jesus was crucified, buried, his tomb was found empty, his disciples saw him after his death, and they were willing to die for that truth.
- ✧ Other explanations, like hallucination or fraud, only explain some of these facts.
- ✧ The most plausible explanation for all these facts is that Jesus really did rise from the dead.

8

Why We Believe in the Trinity

WHEN I WAS walking home after school with my friend Adam I told him about what I'd been discussing with the students at the Catholic youth group.

I said, "So we were talking about Jesus and they think he's God."

"You mean the God who made everything?"

"Yeah."

Adam looked down to ponder this and then said, "But I thought they believed Jesus was the Son of God, not God."

"They do," I replied, "but I'm not sure about the difference. I'll look into it."

Then I hit the books, especially *The Catechism of the Catholic Church*. This is basically the manual that explains what Catholics believe. According to the *Catechism*, Christians believe in one God who exists as a Trinity of three divine persons—the Father, the Son, and the Holy Spirit. It says, "The divine persons do not share the one divinity among themselves but each of them is God whole and entire" (CCC 253).

But how can there be *one* God who is *three* persons? Isn't that a contradiction?

WHAT IS THE TRINITY?

In order to understand the Trinity, we must understand three key words: being, person, and nature.

A *being* is an existing entity, or "*that* something is"; a *person* is a rational individual or "*who* someone is"; and a *nature* refers to "*what* something is." For example, you exist so you are a kind of being (in this case, an animal). You are also a person who has a human nature, that is, you have the capacity to act in distinctly human ways. So you are a *being* who is one *person* and possesses one human *nature*.

DEFINING OUR TERMS:

- **Being**: An existing entity (*that* something is).
- **Person**: A relation or individual capable of reasoning (*who* something is).
- **Nature**: The traits and ends of a certain being (*what* something is).

God is one being that exists as three persons who each fully possess the divine nature.

So how does this relate to God? Christians do not believe God is *one person* with infinite attributes. That belief, held for example by Jews and Muslims, is called unitarianism. Christians believe that God is *one being* who exists as *three persons*, each of whom fully possess the divine *nature*. Christians are not unitarians but trinitarians. They believe that because there is only one God, and the Bible shows that the Father is God, the Son is God, and the Holy Spirit is God, this means the one God must be three persons. Matthew 28:19 hints at this reality when it says that Jesus commanded baptism in the *name* (not names) of the Father, the Son, and the Holy Spirit.

IS THE HOLY SPIRIT GOD?

Many people think the Holy Spirit is just some kind of force, but the Bible describes the Spirit speaking in sentences to people, proving he is a person (Acts 13:2). The Bible also says the Holy Spirit will guide us "into all the truth" (John 16:13), and that the Spirit alone comprehends the thoughts of God (1 Cor. 2:11). Who else but God can know all truth or comprehend God's thoughts?

The apostle Peter shows us that the Holy Spirit is God when he asks Ananias, who lied and held back money due to the apostles, "Ananias, why has Satan filled your heart to lie to the Holy Spirit and to keep back part of the proceeds of the land? . . . You have not lied to men but to God" (Acts 5:3-4).

Not only is the Holy Spirit a person who can be lied to, but lying to the Holy Spirit is the same as lying to God, because the Holy Spirit is the third person of the Trinity.

The Trinity can't be grasped if we think of "beings" and "persons" as the same thing. If we recognize that there are beings that are zero persons (such as rocks and trees) and there are beings that are one person (such as humans and angels), then we see there could be a being that is three persons, or God.

GOD OR *A* GOD?

One way to understand the Trinity is to look at religions that misunderstand it. For example, when I was speaking to two Mormon missionaries, we discussed whether they believed Jesus was God. They said, "Absolutely, Jesus is the Son of God."

I then asked them if they would pray to Jesus. They became visibly uncomfortable and said, "No, Mormons don't do that."

The reason Mormons don't pray to Jesus is because they believe the Trinity is a collection of three separate divine beings, not three persons in one being, and that the Father created the Son and the Holy Spirit.[53] They even believe Jesus is our "eldest brother," and if we follow what the Mormon Church teaches we will become "gods," just like Jesus and the Father "became gods" at one point in the past.[54] This, of course, contradicts the evidence we discussed earlier, which shows that the Creator of the universe must exist without limit and so there can be only one infinite God. It also contradicts the testimony of Scripture, which says there is only one God (Deut. 4:39, Isa. 45:5, John 17:3).[55]

After hearing this, I told the missionaries, "I appreciate that you're trying to share your faith, but I love being a Christian. The reason I could never become a Mormon is because I would miss the relationship I have with Jesus Christ. I love praying to Jesus and knowing he isn't 'a god' but, as the apostle Thomas said, 'My Lord and my God'" (John 20:28).

Jehovah's Witnesses also deny the Trinity because they believe there is only one "true" or "mighty God," who is the Father. They say Jesus is just "a god" the Father created, because Jesus said, "the Father is greater than I" (John 14:28). But when Jesus said this he meant the Father was greater than him in *position* since, at that time, the Father gloriously reigned in heaven while Jesus humbly ministered on earth.

When God the Son became man, he was made "lower than the angels" (Heb. 2:9), but Jesus was not an exalted man or some kind of angel. (Jehovah's Witnesses think Jesus and Michael the archangel are the same person.)[56] Hebrews 1:4-6 says Jesus has

> become as much superior to angels as the name he has obtained is more excellent than theirs. For to what angel did God ever say, "Thou art my Son, today I have begotten thee"? Or again, "I will be to him a father, and he shall be to me a son"? And again, when he brings the first-born into the world, he says, "*Let all God's angels worship him*" (emphasis added).[57]

Angels don't worship other angels; they worship only God. But if the son of a dog is a dog, and the son of man is a man, then the son of God must be God. If there is only one God, then God must exist as more than one person that can be worshipped: the Father, Son, and Holy Spirit.

CAN GOD DIE?

Some people ask, "How can Jesus be God if he prayed to God? How can Jesus be God if he died on a cross?"

Saying that "Jesus is God" means Jesus is a divine person, one of three divine persons who belong to the Trinity. The Father and the Holy Spirit did not become man, but the Son did. In doing so Jesus remained one divine *person*, with a fully *divine nature*, but he also assumed an additional *human nature*. Therefore, whatever is true of Jesus is also true of God, even if it may sound strange at first. For example, since Jesus died on the cross, it is also true that God died on the cross, because Jesus is God.

Of course, God did not *go out of existence*, but that is not what it means to die. Death occurs when a living being's parts are separated into their basic elements, or they decompose. Jesus' soul was separated from his body, so Jesus, the God-man, died. Jesus did not go out of existence, but his soul did exist apart from his body. However, through Jesus' divine nature, he was able to reunite his body and soul and raise himself from the dead.[58] God died on the cross, but he also rose from the dead to glorious eternal life.

Likewise, when Jesus prayed to God he wasn't talking to himself—he was praying to the Father. Since God is more than one person, there is no contradiction in God the Son becoming man and praying to the Father who is in heaven. God is our father by adoption (Rom. 8:15), but Jesus' father by nature (John 1:18), since both the Father and the Son are equally divine. In fact, the Bible tells us that the Jews wanted to stone Jesus because he "called God his Father, making himself equal with God" (John 5:18).

ONE PERSON OR THREE PERSONS?

Another misunderstanding occurs when people say that the Trinity is like one man being a father, husband, and son at the same time. This is not trinitarianism, but the heresy of modalism, which says that the Trinity is made up of three aspects or *modes* of God, each of which has a different role. This is very popular among so-called "Jesus-only" Christians or Oneness Pentecostals.

They say there is only one God and God manifests himself as the Father at some times, and the Son and Holy Spirit at other times. But this doesn't make sense of Scripture passages that describe Jesus talking to the Father (John 17), saying he will return to the Father (John 14:12), or that the Son will send the Holy Spirit in his place (John 14:16-17, Acts 2:33).

Since my husbandness and fatherness can't talk to each other, this means the Son of God is not a "role" God plays. He is a person who God is, or the person of Jesus Christ. God is not one person but one being that is three coequal, coeternal persons.

A PAGAN INFLUENCE?

Some Jehovah's Witnesses say that the first Christians did not believe in the Trinity. They say when Christianity became the official religion of the Roman Empire in the fourth century, pagan converts brought this heretical idea about God with them. But a hundred years earlier the ecclesial writer Tertullian said, "The unity is distributed in a Trinity. Placed in order, the three are the Father, Son, and Spirit."[59]

Although it is a mystery ultimately beyond our human reason, the doctrine of the Trinity is not just some piece of theological trivia. Indeed, this doctrine demonstrates one of God's most amazing attributes: that he is *love* (1 John 4:8).

God is not a solitary being who has existed by himself from eternity past. As love itself, God is a relationship of persons who eternally give and receive love among one another. God's love is so unending that he desires to share it with each of us, a point Jesus made when he said, "If a man loves me, he will keep my word, and my Father will love him, and we will come to him and make our home with him" (John 14:23).

WHY WE BELIEVE: THE TRINITY

✧ The Bible teaches that there is only one God.

✧ The Father, Son, and Holy Spirit are three distinct persons who share the same divine nature—that is, each of them is God.

✧ Therefore, God is one being that exists as a Trinity of three coequal, coeternal divine persons.

9

Why We Believe in the Bible

ONCE WHEN I was speaking at a university, a young man asked me, "How can you believe in the Bible when it contradicts science and says you'll be stoned to death if you break a law in the Old Testament? It even commands people to kill each other. How can you believe in all that stuff?!"

I looked at him for a moment and then said, "Those are great questions and I'm happy to explain my answer to each one of them, but the main reason I believe in the Bible is because Jesus believed in the Bible. If a guy can walk out of his own tomb, then I trust his judgment."

I then told him that the Bible is the word of God, but God allowed many different human authors to write the seventy-three different books that make up the Bible. Those authors only wrote what God wanted, but God allowed them to use their own styles and human perspectives in what they wrote. We must take that into account and not read the Bible as if it were an instruction manual God wrote and shipped down from heaven.

> **The Bible is fully divine in its inspiration and fully human in its composition, free from error and written so we might be saved from sin.**

I then spent a few minutes sharing with this young man the "big picture" of what the Bible teaches.

CREATION AND COVENANTS

The Bible (named from the Greek word for "book") is a collection of books and letters, written over a period of centuries, that describe God's revelation to man and man's response to that revelation. Also called Sacred Scripture, the Bible is divided into two main parts: the Old Testament and the New Testament.

The first book of the Bible, Genesis, teaches that God created the world and made human beings in his image. The beginning of this book is written in the style of epic poetry, so its description of the creation of the world in six days is not scientific in nature. For example, Genesis describes how God created "light" on the first day, but created the sun, the thing that even ancient people knew makes the light, on the fourth day. This can be explained if the author of Genesis was using poetic, nonliteral language instead of a chronological, literal description of the Creation.

An example of a true, nonliteral description would be when a parent explains to his child that babies "come from a seed daddy gives to mommy that grows inside the mommy's tummy." That's a true description; it just shouldn't be taken literally. The Catholic Church teaches that the book of Genesis also truthfully describes the Creation of the world, but it does so through the use of nonliteral language.[60]

Genesis also describes how our first parents rebelled against

God and how God progressively revealed himself to human beings in order to save humanity from sin and death. These include the formation of *covenants*, or sacred pledges of loyalty, which God made with men like Noah and Abraham, the latter of whom became the father of God's chosen people, Israel. In Egypt, archaeologists discovered a large granite stone from the year 1208 B.C., called the Merneptah Stele, that refers to the existence of Israel.[61] God decreed that this group of people, named after Abraham's grandson, would bless the entire world.

A PEOPLE BECOMES A NATION

The next books of the Bible describe how Israel was enslaved in Egypt until God formed a covenant with Moses. Moses led Israel to freedom out of Egypt and into the desert, where they wandered for forty years. They eventually settled in the land God had promised them, in an area called Canaan (located in modern-day Israel).

During this time God gave his people laws that modern readers sometimes don't understand, such as rules that forbid eating pork or mixing fabrics. Only some of these laws (like "Thou shall not murder") are binding on believers today. The other "purity" laws like "Thou shall not eat pork" were only meant for ancient Israel, but they served an important purpose.

They were designed to keep Israel separate from other nations that might tempt them to worship pagan gods who practiced incest, promoted prostitution, and demanded child sacrifice by fire. The laws that forbade Israelites from eating certain foods or wearing certain clothes helped them see that they should not imitate other nations, but remain unique and "pure" in their worship and love of God.

Here's an analogy to help understand this distinction. When I was a child, my mom gave me two rules: hold her hand when I cross the street and don't drink from the bottles under the sink. The purity laws were like mom's hand-holding rule. They helped the Israelites understand the discipline God's law requires and protected them from destructive pagan influences (just as hand-holding protected me from careless drivers). Moral laws, on the other hand, deal with things that are always harmful, like murder or adultery, and so Christians still follow them even though they are found in the Old Testament (just as I still follow the rule "If it's under the sink, don't drink!").

A NATION GOES TO WAR

The first five books of the Bible, which Jewish people call the Torah and scholars call the Pentateuch, end with the death of Moses and the installation of his successor, Joshua. The book of Joshua continues Israel's story and describes how Israel contended with the hostile tribes that inhabited the land of Canaan (the Canaanites). Some of these descriptions include commands to wipe out entire nations, which are very disturbing. But since God gave us our lives, he alone has the authority to end them at any time and in any way. This would include using his chosen people to carry out a judgment against a culture known for its unparalleled wickedness and evil.

ANCIENT CHILD SACRIFICE

God's people were forbidden to offer human sacrifices, but such sacrifices were common among the Canaanites, which resulted in God's judgment against them. Here's how one ancient historian describes these sacrifices:

"There stands in their midst a bronze statue of Kronos, its hands extended over a bronze brazier, the flames of which engulf the child. When the flames fall upon the body, the limbs contract and the open mouth seems almost to be laughing, until the contracted [body] slips quietly into the brazier."[62]

It could also be the case that the language used in these texts is exaggerated, nonliteral "warfare rhetoric." This kind of language is akin to saying your favorite sports team "destroyed" or "massacred" its opponents. Ancient battle accounts also use this language, which can be seen in the Merneptah Stele. It says that Israel was "laid waste and his seed is not," even though the nation of Israel continued to exist for several centuries after the stele was erected.

The fact that the book of Judges describes these same hostile nations existing after they were "utterly destroyed" shows that other books of the Bible, like Joshua, probably used exaggerated language. The author's point was that Israel could not absorb any part of the nations they fought, but must "utterly destroy them." Tolerating any part of such a destructive culture would result in God's people falling into the same kind of wickedness.

A KINGDOM AND AN EXILE

Along with books that tell the story of God's people, the Old Testament (or Hebrew Bible) contains literature that teaches God's people wisdom and right living, such as the book of Proverbs. It also contains collections of prayers and hymns, like those found in the book of Psalms. Other books in the Old Testament include stories that were written to teach people how to have faith in God, such as the story of Job, who kept his faith in spite of tremendous suffering.

The remaining historical books of the Old Testament, for example, Samuel and Kings, describe how Israel became a kingdom and then a divided kingdom. The most famous of Israel's kings was David, who most people remember as the shepherd boy who defeated the Philistine giant, Goliath, with a sling and a stone. David's son Solomon succeeded him, but Solomon's inability to keep God's people from falling into idolatry and wickedness led to the nation being divided into northern and southern kingdoms.

It's important to remember that just because the Bible *records* God's people being wicked or doing evil things doesn't mean God *recommends* those practices. These evil actions are what motivated God to send a series of prophets to urge his people to repent and turn away from their sins. The prophets told the people to care for widows and orphans (who were at risk of starving to death), not to worship idols, and not to engage in wicked sexual behavior.

Unfortunately, these prophetic reforms were either ignored or did not last. As a result, other nations conquered the northern and southern kingdoms and took God's people into captivity. The final historical books of the Old Testament reveal how God's people were freed from captivity and returned to their promised land. Unfortunately, even after their return, God's people suffered under the rule of foreign powers like the Greeks (and later the Romans). Through all of this they patiently awaited the Messiah: a savior promised in Scripture who would restore God's kingdom.

"Ignorance of Scripture is ignorance of Christ." —*St. Jerome, a fourth-century Bible scholar who produced the world's most popular Latin translation of the Bible*

A SAVIOR IS BORN

The New Testament is the story of that Messiah, Jesus Christ (Christ is a title for the Messiah that means "anointed one"). The four Gospels (Matthew, Mark, Luke, and John) tell us that Jesus existed as the Son of God before the creation of the world and that he became man in order to save humanity from its sins. The Gospels end after Christ's resurrection, when he commissioned his followers to become apostles (a Greek word that means "messenger"). Their mission was to share the good news of Christ's resurrection and offer of salvation with the entire world.

The Acts of the Apostles is the book that picks up where the Gospels leave off. (Its author also wrote the Gospel of Luke.) It describes how after Jesus ascended into heaven, the Church he created flourished in spite of the persecution it faced from Jewish and Roman leaders. The rest of the New Testament includes a collection of letters the apostles sent to various communities in order to teach and encourage them to keep the Faith.

The last book of the Bible is Revelation, which contains visions of God's heavenly kingdom. Revelation also contains prophecies about the end of the world and describes how God will conquer evil. After God's victory he will gather his people, both the living and the dead, to himself, in order to share glorious, eternal life with him.

THE CHURCH AND THE BIBLE

It's a circular argument to say the Bible is the word of God because the Bible says it is the word of God. That assumes what you're trying to prove. But we've seen that even if we assume the Bible is a collection of human documents, they still provide historical evidence that a man, Jesus Christ, rose from the dead.

They also show that Jesus established a Church built on apostles to whom he gave spiritual authority (Matt 16:18–19, Eph. 2:20). Christ told the apostles, "He who hears you, hears me" (Luke 10:16). But this authority did not end when the apostles died. The successors of the apostles, the future bishops of the Church, inherited this spiritual authority and were able to declare the Bible to be the word of God.

This is not a circular argument, in which an inspired Bible is used to prove the Church's authority and the Church's authority is used to prove that the Bible is inspired. Instead, it is a "spiral argument," in which the Bible is assumed to be a merely human document that records the creation of a divinely instituted Church.[63] This Church then had the authority to pronounce which human writings also had God as their author. The great fourth-century theologian St. Augustine reached a similar conclusion when he said, "I should not believe the gospel except as moved by the authority of the Catholic Church."[64]

WHY WE BELIEVE: THE BIBLE

✧ The Old Testament describes God's creation of the world, man's fall into sin, and the restoration of God's family through his chosen people, Israel.

✧ The New Testament describes the coming of the Messiah, Jesus Christ, the divine Son of God who expanded God's family to include the whole world by dying on a cross and atoning for humanity's sins.

✧ Christ established the Catholic Church to be the custodian of his revelation, and from it we have the Bible that Christians read today.

10

Why We Aren't Bible-Only Christians

After I became a Christian I struggled with whether I should keep attending a Catholic Church. As I sat in church and watched incense rise up from the altar, I felt an urge to stay and be part of what felt like a sacred mystery. On the other hand, there were a lot of Catholic beliefs that I could not find in the Bible, which made me think they were just man-made traditions.

I eventually decided that it didn't matter which church I joined so long as I only believed in what the Bible taught. But then I ran into a roadblock: I couldn't find a single Bible verse that said everything I believed had to be found in the Bible. And the more I studied history, the more I saw it was the *Catholic Church* that gave us the Bible.

If I believed in God's word, then why wouldn't I join the Church that gave us this word in the form of Sacred Scripture?

THE UNBIBLICAL IDEA OF *SOLA SCRIPTURA*

In the sixteenth century, Christians like Martin Luther and John Calvin opposed what they thought were "man-made traditions" of the Catholic Church. Because of their protest against the Church, they came to be known as the *Protestant Reformers*. However, instead of reforming the Catholic Church, they rejected the Church's authority and replaced it with the idea that all Christian teaching, or doctrine, should come from the Bible alone. This principle later came to be called *sola scriptura* (Latin for "by Scripture alone").

But if all doctrine is supposed to come from the Bible, then where does the Bible teach the doctrine of *sola scriptura*?

It's true that Revelation 22:18 warns that "everyone who hears the words of the prophecy of this book: if any one adds to them, God will add to him the plagues described in this book." But John, the author of Revelation, was just prohibiting the addition of words to the visions he received. He was not denying that the word of God exists outside the Bible, or even outside his own revelation.

The passage most often cited in defense of *sola scriptura* is 2 Timothy 3:16-17: "All Scripture is inspired by God and profitable for teaching, for reproof, for correction, and for training in righteousness, that the man of God may be complete, equipped for every good work."[65]

Catholics agree that all Scripture is inspired by God. Scripture is also useful, but this doesn't mean Scripture is the *only* thing that helps us teach the Faith or grow in holiness. We also need an active prayer life and advice from other mature Christians. In 2 Timothy 2:21, Paul says that if Timothy cleanses himself from bad influences he will be a vessel ready for "any good work." Of course, that doesn't mean that if Timothy stays away from bad influences he will automatically know every essential doctrine of the Faith.

The Bible teaches that Scripture is *one* tool that equips us to do good works, but it is not the only tool that makes us ready for that task. In fact, the Bible teaches that God's word is not restricted to the written word alone.

THE NECESSITY OF TRADITION

The first Christians didn't learn their faith from the Bible because none of the books of the New Testament had been written yet. This is evident in Paul thanking the Corinthians for "maintain[ing] the traditions even as I have delivered them to you" (1 Cor. 11:2), and instructing his disciple Timothy, "what you have heard from me before many witnesses entrust to faithful men who will be able to teach others also" (2 Tim. 2:2).

Paul thanked the Thessalonians for accepting his preaching, not as human words, but as the very words of God (1 Thess. 2:13). In his second letter to this community he told them to "stand firm and hold to the traditions which you were taught by us, either by word of mouth or by letter" (2 Thess. 2:15).

TRADITION AND TRADITIONS DEFINED

- **Ecclesial tradition**: The rules and customs taught by the Church that aid us in worshipping God. These include styles of worship or rules that can change when it is most helpful for the Body of Christ.
- **Sacred Tradition**: The word of God in oral form that Jesus and the apostles entrusted to the Church and that do not change. These include basic doctrines of the Faith and ways of living out the Faith in every generation.

Sacred Tradition is not the same as customs that can change over time, like manner of dress or style of worship (or "tradition" with a lowercase "t").[66] Tradition (with a capital "T") refers to the word of God that is "handed on" or "delivered." It does not change even though our understanding of it grows over time, in the same way our understanding of Scripture grows over time.

In the second century, St. Irenaeus wrote, "While the languages of the world are diverse, nevertheless, the authority of the tradition is one and the same." He also asked his readers, "What if the apostles had not in fact left writings to us? Would it not be necessary to follow the order of tradition, which was handed down to those to whom they entrusted the churches?"[67]

TRADITIONS OF MEN?

Some Christians object to the idea of Sacred Tradition because they believe Jesus condemned it. They refer to the time when Jesus told the Jewish leaders, "For the sake of your tradition, you have made void the word of God" (Matt. 15:6). But in this case Jesus was condemning a particular man-made tradition that was contrary to one of God's commandments. Specifically, Jesus criticized the tradition of applying a sacrificial offering of money, called *korban,* to the Temple instead of using the money to support one's elderly parents. This tradition contradicted the Fourth Commandment, which says, "Honor your father and mother."

However, Jesus did not reject religious tradition as a whole because he told his disciples to obey the Jewish leaders because they sat on something called "Moses' seat" (Matt. 23:2-3). This was not an actual chair but a term that referred to a Jewish tradition, not found in Scripture, about the Jewish leaders' teaching authority. In fact, prior to his Ascension into heaven Jesus never commanded the apostles to write anything down. Instead, their mission was to preach the gospel, and the word of God continued to be passed down in oral tradition even after the New Testament was written.

THE BIBLE'S TABLE OF CONTENTS

The clearest example of a Sacred Tradition that both Catholics and Protestants accept is the canon of Scripture. The word "canon" comes from a Greek word that means "rule," and refers to the Church's official list of inspired writings. You can find this list in the table of contents of every Catholic or Protestant Bible. The canon of Scripture was first declared in Rome in A.D. 382 and was later defined at two Catholic councils in North Africa (Hippo in A.D. 393 and Carthage in A.D. 397).[68]

A PROTESTANT THEOLOGIAN ADMITS: THERE'S A PROBLEM

"The problem with contemporary Protestants is that they have no doctrine of the Table of Contents. With the approach that is popular in conservative evangelical circles, one simply comes to the Bible by means of an epistemological lurch. The Bible 'just is,' and any questions about how it got here are dismissed as a nuisance. But time passes, the questions remain unanswered, the silence becomes awkward, and conversions of thoughtful evangelicals to Rome proceed apace."[69]

—Protestant theologian Douglas Wilson

However, if you are a Christian who denies the authority of the Catholic Church, then by what authority can you say Christians must accept the canon of Scripture found in today's Bibles?

Some say it's just obvious the books of the Bible all belong there and we don't need any Church to prove they do, but is it really so obvious? Paul's letter to Philemon doesn't teach any specific doctrine, and the third letter of John doesn't even mention the name of Jesus Christ. Conversely, other writings that were popular in the early Church, like the *Didache* or the letter of Clement, are not in the canon of Scripture[70]

Others say "the church" (with a lowercase "c") determined the canon, but we aren't obligated to follow what any church might teach today. But if that group of early Christians did not have Christ's authority, then we have no reason to continue following their doctrinal decisions, including their decisions about the canon. The Protestant theologian R.C. Sproul famously suggested that the best we can say is that the canon of Scripture is "a fallible list of infallible books."[71] This means any Christian who feels moved by the Holy Spirit could claim the table of contents in the Bible needs to be revised, or even that some portions of the Bible should be removed.[72]

In fact, 500 years ago Martin Luther and other Protestant Reformers did just that. Luther called the letter of James "an epistle of straw" because it contradicted his theology, so he moved it to the back of the Bible. Even though Luther and the other Reformers kept the letter of James, they removed books, called the *deuterocanonicals,* from the Old Testament. These books, like Sirach, Tobit, and Maccabees (among others), were part of the Bible Jesus used and were considered inspired Scripture in the early Church.[73] One reason the Reformers rejected books was because they teach Catholic doctrines like the existence of purgatory and the need to pray for the dead.[74]

SCRIPTURE, TRADITION, AND THE CHURCH

Catholics agree we should not believe anything that contradicts God's word, in either its written form (the Bible) or its oral form (Tradition).

If an alleged tradition contradicts Scripture, then the tradition must be of human—small "t"—rather than divine—capital "T"—origin. But if a document that claims to be Scripture (such as a forged or heretical gospel) contradicts Sacred Tradition, then it, too, must be of human origin. God speaks through the written word, but as we've seen, only through Scared Tradition can we know which writings are the word of God and which ones are not.

Sacred Tradition also protects the Church from *false interpretations* of the Bible. My Protestant friends would sometimes debate other religious people who denied basic Christian doctrines like the deity of Christ. They would point out Bible passages that they say proved Jesus is God, only to hear the other person say, "Yes, but that's not how *I* interpret those passages." I thought it was ironic when one of my Protestant friends said, "But my interpretation of these passages is the same one Christians have held for 2,000 years!"

This was a perfect example of how God's word speaks in Scripture through the written word (or what the Bible *says*), but also through oral Tradition (or teachings about what the Bible *means*). But whose tradition should we look to for guidance on interpreting the Bible?

My Protestant friends couldn't even agree among themselves on what the Bible taught concerning issues such as whether babies should be baptized or if salvation can be lost. It's no wonder that in his second letter St. Peter taught, "no prophecy of Scripture is a matter of one's own interpretation" (2 Pet. 1:20).

St. Vincent of Lerins made this point in the fifth century when he noticed that heretics could cite Scripture just as well as the faithful. This meant that another authority was necessary to settle disputes about what Christians should believe. This authority could be none other than the Church Christ founded, or, as Vincent wrote, "The rule for the right understanding of the prophets and apostles should be framed in accordance with the standard of ecclesiastical and Catholic interpretation."[75]

WHY WE BELIEVE: THE BIBLE AND TRADITION

- The Bible never teaches that God's word is confined to the written word or that everything Christians believe is explicitly described in the Bible.

- The Bible teaches that God's word exists in oral form as Sacred Tradition.

- One tradition that both Catholics and Protestants believe in is the canon of Scripture.

PART 3

The CHURCH & the SACRAMENTS

11

Why We Belong to the Catholic Church

WHEN I WAS considering joining the Catholic Church, I sat down with some of my non-Catholic friends to see if they could talk me out of my decision. They were Christians, but they didn't consider themselves to be "Protestants." Instead, they called themselves Evangelicals or just "Christ-followers." Regardless, their response to my decision to become Catholic surprised me.

One of the girls said, "As long as Catholics believe in Jesus then I don't think it's a big deal." Another chimed in, "I mean, we're never going to know which church is the right church or even if there is such a thing, so why worry?"

That answer didn't satisfy me so I asked them, "Don't you wonder if one of the churches that exists today can be traced back to the Church Jesus founded? Don't you wonder which church *Jesus* wants us to join?"

THE FIRST CHRISTIANS

My question was met with a collective shrug and a simple recommendation that I just "believe in Jesus," but that wasn't good enough for me. How did my Evangelical friends know we only have to believe in Jesus to be saved? What does it *mean* to believe in Jesus? Do we have to be baptized to believe in Jesus? Do we have to receive Communion? If I stop believing in Jesus will I lose my salvation?

I wanted the answers to these questions so I decided to study what the very first Christians believed. These were the believers who lived just after the apostles. If there was one church I wanted to belong to, it was their church.

In the time of the apostles believers were called "Christians," but the Church was not called "the Christian Church." It was simply referred to as "the Church," as is evident in Luke's description of what Paul and Barnabas did in the city of Antioch. He said, "For a whole year they met with the Church, and taught a large company of people; and in Antioch the disciples were for the first time called Christians" (Acts 11:26).

A few decades later, St. Ignatius of Antioch wrote a letter to Christians who lived 600 miles away, in the coastal city of Smyrna (located in modern Turkey). He said, "Wherever the bishop shall appear, there let the multitude [of the people] also be; even as, wherever Jesus Christ is, there is the Catholic Church."[76]

WHO STARTED YOUR CHURCH?

- ✦ Calvary Chapel, 1965: Chuck Smith
- ✦ Mormon church, 1830: Joseph Smith
- ✦ Disciples of Christ, 1809: Thomas Campbell

- ✦ Baptist church, 1609: John Smyth
- ✦ Presbyterian church, 1560: John Knox
- ✦ Calvinist church, 1536: John Calvin
- ✦ Lutheran church, 1517: Martin Luther
- ✦ Eastern Orthodox church, 1054: Eastern Patriarchs
- ✦ Catholic Church, 33: Jesus Christ

The word Catholic comes from the Greek word *kataholos*, which means "according to" (*kata*) "the whole" (*holos*). Christ's Church is called the Catholic Church because it is the same Church regardless of where or when it is found. The Church is the same because it contains the fullness of God's eternal plan of salvation for the human race.

WHAT IS THE CHURCH?

St. Paul says the Church was built on "the foundation of the apostles" (Eph. 2:20) and is "the pillar and bulwark of the truth" (1 Tim. 3:15). Jesus said the gates of hell would not prevail against the Church, and that the apostles, especially Peter, would have authority over it (Matt. 16:18–19, 18:17). If the apostles alone had the authority to speak on Christ's behalf (Luke 10:16), then that authority would be lost once they all died. Fortunately, God gave the apostles the ability to pass on their spiritual authority to worthy successors.

After the death of Judas (the apostle who betrayed Jesus), Peter proclaimed that Judas's position among the apostles would be transferred to a worthy successor (Acts 1:20). St. Paul even warned Timothy, "Do not be hasty in the laying on of hands" when he appointed new leaders in the Church

(1 Tim. 5:22). The apostles did all this to make sure their authority to "bind and loose" (Matt. 18:18), that is, to determine Church teaching and practice, would be passed on to their successors.

In A.D. 110 St. Ignatius of Antioch told his readers, "Follow the bishop, even as Jesus Christ does the Father, and the presbytery [or priests] as you would the apostles; and reverence the deacons, as being the institution of God. Let no man do anything connected with the Church without the bishop."[77]

THE FOURTH POPE SPEAKS

At the end of the first century, the fourth pope, Clement, reminded the Christians in the city of Corinth about the reality of apostolic succession, saying,

> Our apostles knew through our Lord Jesus Christ that there would be strife for the office of bishop. For this reason, therefore, having received perfect foreknowledge, they appointed those who have already been mentioned and afterward added the further provision that, if they should die, other approved men should succeed to their ministry.[78]

AN OLD BABY PHOTO

"How can today's Catholic Church with all of its traditions and rituals be the same humble Church we read about in the New Testament?" It's a good question, but it's sort of like asking, "How can that fully grown man be the same little boy whose diaper had to be changed decades earlier?" In both cases the body being described grew and developed over time without becoming a different kind of being.

The man, for example, has some things he did not have as a

baby (like whiskers). But he also has many things he did have as a baby. This includes the same DNA that guides his growth and gives him features like "his father's nose," which can be seen in his old baby photos. In the same way, the Catholic Church, which St. Paul calls the Body of Christ (Eph. 5:23), has the same "DNA" as the Church of the first century: the word of God. This word is transmitted both through Sacred Scripture and Sacred Tradition, and you can see its effect in one of the Church's "old baby photos."

One particular "photo" comes from the second century, when St. Justin Martyr wrote about how when Christians gathered to worship, they "offer hearty prayers in common for ourselves and for the baptized person, and for all others in every place." After that, they "salute one another with a kiss," the presider at the service takes bread and wine and does the following:

> [He] gives praise and glory to the Father of the universe, through the name of the Son and of the Holy Ghost, and offers thanks at considerable length for our being counted worthy to receive these things at His hands. And when he has concluded the prayers and thanksgivings, all the people present express their assent by saying Amen.[79]

Justin's description corresponds to the prayers of the faithful, the exchange of peace, the offering of bread and wine, and the "great amen" that are still said at Catholic services today. Justin goes on to say that the bread and wine at Mass are not mere symbols of Christ's body and blood, but are instead "the flesh and blood of that Jesus who was made flesh." This doctrine, the Real Presence of Christ in the Eucharist, is one the Catholic Church still teaches and defends (see chapter 14 for more).

Here are some other examples of what the first Christians believed. Can you see the resemblance to what Catholics believe today in these other "baby photos"?

✧ Submit to the bishop as you would to Jesus Christ. —*St. Ignatius, A.D. 110.*[80]

✧ Happy is our sacrament of water, in that, by washing away the sins of our early blindness, we are set free and admitted into eternal life. —*Tertullian, A.D. 203.*[81]

✧ The Church received from the apostles the tradition of giving baptism even to infants. —*Origen, A.D. 248.*[82]

✧ Of how much greater faith and salutary fear are they who ... confess their sins to the priests of God in a straightforward manner. —*St Cyprian, A.D. 251.*[83]

IS CATHOLICISM PAGAN?

Some people claim that in the late fourth century, when Christianity became the official religion of the Roman Empire, non-Christians converted purely out of convenience. These new converts brought with them "man-made rituals" that corrupted Christ's Church. But as we've seen, doctrines like the priesthood, the real presence of Christ in the Eucharist, and the sacrament of confession were believed long before the fourth century and can even be traced back to what Jesus and the apostles taught.

It's true the Catholic Church took what was good in non-Catholic religions and used it to glorify God, but all Christians do this. The custom of exchanging rings at a wedding, for example, was first practiced in ancient Egypt and is not described in the Bible. Of course, the meaning of the ritual does not contradict what the Church teaches about marriage. In fact, the never-ending nature of rings symbolizes the permanence of marriage, which is why even Protestants usually have this "pagan" custom at their wedding services.

If Catholic customs like burning incense, lighting candles, and singing chants contain unforgivable infusions of "paganism" into the Church, then Protestant churches that use fog machines, stage lights, and popular music in their services would be just as pagan. Pope St. John Paul II taught that using cultural elements in service of the gospel is not wrong as long as such elements "in no way compromise the distinctiveness and integrity of the Christian faith."[84]

WHO WILL SHOW ME?

The book of Acts describes how a servant of the queen of Ethiopia was puzzled when he read the prophecies of the Old Testament.[85] Fortunately, Philip the evangelist came along and asked the servant, "Do you understand what you are reading?" The servant replied, "How can I, unless someone guides me?" Philip showed the servant how the Old Testament's promised Messiah was Jesus Christ. He then baptized the servant in a nearby pool of water (Acts 8:26-40).

Many people feel just as confused as the Ethiopian servant when they read the Bible. St. Peter even warned his readers that there are confusing passages in Scripture, whose meaning some people twist to their own destruction (2 Peter 3:16). If that's true, then wouldn't Jesus make sure someone like Philip was still around today to help people understand what they're reading in God's word? The Bible does not say there should be hundreds of competing denominations that each have different interpretations of the Bible. Instead, it says, "There is one body and one Spirit . . . one Lord, one faith, one baptism" (Eph. 4:4-5).

The *Catechism* teaches that through baptism all Christians are "put in a certain, although imperfect, communion with the Catholic Church" (CCC 838). What Catholics desire is for their non-Catholic friends to have a *perfect* communion with Christ's Church. That way every Christian can fulfill Jesus' prayer that all his followers "may be one," just as he and the Father are one (John 17:11).

ST. AUGUSTINE ON BEING CATHOLIC

St. Augustine was the fourth-century bishop of Hippo who became one of the most famous theologians in the history of Christianity. Many Protestants even seek to follow his teachings, as is evident in John Calvin's remark that "Augustine is so wholly with me, that if I wished to write a confession of my faith, I could do so with all fullness and satisfaction to myself out of his writings."[86] In his letter to the heretic Mani, however, Augustine revealed what keeps him in the Catholic Church.

"The succession of priests, from the very see of the apostle Peter, to whom the Lord, after his resurrection, gave the charge of feeding his sheep (John 21:15-17), up to the present episcopate, keeps me here. And last, the very name Catholic, which, not without reason, belongs to this Church alone, in the face of so many heretics, so much so that, although all heretics want to be called 'Catholic,' when a stranger inquires where the Catholic Church meets, none of the heretics would dare to point out his own basilica or house."[87]

WHY WE BELIEVE: THE CATHOLIC CHURCH

- ✧ Jesus established a Church built on the apostles that included a hierarchy, or sacred order, that included deacons, priests, and bishops.

- ✧ Only the Catholic Church can trace its authority back to the apostles and their immediate successors.

- ✧ The Catholic Church maintains in its current teachings the ancient doctrines of Christ, the apostles, and the early Church.

12

Why We Have a Pope

LET'S TRAVEL FORWARD in time about ten years after my conversion to the Catholic faith. It was 4:45 a.m., and my wife and I were standing in a subway station outside of Rome waiting for the train to arrive. The handful of people on the platform couldn't help but stare at my wife pacing back and forth in her long, flowing wedding dress. Both of us were wearing our wedding attire because newly married couples are allowed to sit in a special section at St. Peter's Basilica, where they have the chance to meet the pope.

We were told that the pope usually just waves to newlyweds after his morning address, which is why we were shocked when a security official pointed to the middle of the platform, in front of an audience of 50,000 people, and told us, "You go there to see pope."

My stomach felt as if it was full of pins and needles, and when the pope finally met us I was at a loss for words. My wife skipped past the formalities and gave him a hug, which the pope's security detail was not happy about (though the pope seemed to have a good laugh over it).

Even our non-Catholic friends get excited when they hear we met the pope, but why is the pope so important to Catholics? The answer is because Christ has entrusted the pope, the bishop of Rome, with the office he first entrusted to St. Peter—to be the pastor of his entire Church.

This man is called "pope" because that word comes from a Latin word for "father" (*papa*). Just as St. Paul said he became a father to the Christians in the Greek city of Corinth (1 Cor. 4:15), the pope is a spiritual father to all believers. He has been entrusted with the same responsibilities Christ gave to Peter, which include spiritually feeding Christ's flock of believers (John 21:15-19) and determining doctrine and practice for Christ's Church (Matt. 16:18-19).

PETER THE LEADER

Peter's role as "chief apostle" is evident in the fact that he is mentioned more than any other apostle, often speaks for the whole group, and is placed first in almost every list of the apostles (Matt. 10:2). We know these lists were made in order of importance because Judas is always listed last.

The book of Acts also describes Peter's unparalleled leadership in the early Church, including his authority to make a binding declaration at the Council of Jerusalem (Acts 15). As the non-Catholic scholar J.N.D. Kelly put it, "Peter was the undisputed leader of the youthful church."[88]

PETER LEADS THE CHURCH

- ✦ The first apostle to see the risen Jesus (Luke 24:34, 1 Cor. 15:5)
- ✦ Preached the first sermon and received the first converts (Acts 2:14-41)
- ✦ Performed the first healing in the Church age (Acts 3:6-10)

- ✦ Excommunicated the first heretic (Acts 8:18-24)
- ✦ Received the first revelation about the Gentiles (Acts 10:44-48)
- ✦ Gave the first binding declaration of dogma for the entire Church (Acts 15:7-11)

Jesus also gave Peter his name, which had previously been Simon. This is important, because in the Bible when God changes someone's name he also changes that person's destiny. For example, Abram's destiny was to be the father of the Jewish people, so God changed his name to Abraham, which means "father of many nations." The name "Peter" means "rock," which meant Peter's destiny was to be some kind of rock or foundation. Jesus revealed just what kind of rock he would be after Peter correctly identified Jesus as "the Christ, the Son of the living God." Jesus said:

> Blessed are you, Simon Bar-Jona! For flesh and blood has not revealed this to you, but my Father who is in heaven. And I tell you, you are Peter, and on this rock I will build my Church, and the powers of death shall not prevail against it. I will give you the keys of the kingdom of heaven, and whatever you bind on earth shall be bound in heaven, and whatever you loose on earth shall be loosed in heaven (Matt. 16:17-19).

In the ancient world, cities were surrounded by giant walls and could only be entered through a massive gate. The ruler of the city was given a large key to this gate, which was also a symbol of his authority over the city. When Jesus gave Peter "the keys of the kingdom," he was alluding to a passage in the Old Testament book of Isaiah that describes how Hezekiah, the king of Israel, gave Eliakim the authority to oversee his entire kingdom. According to Isaiah 22:22, Eliakim would have "the key of the house of David; he shall open, and none shall shut; and he shall shut, and none shall open."

Jesus told the apostles, "as my Father appointed a kingdom for me, so do I appoint for you" (Luke 22:29). Like any responsible Jewish king, Jesus selected one person, the apostle Peter, to oversee this kingdom as his prime minister.[89] As the Protestant scholar Craig Keener writes in his commentary on Matthew, "[Jesus] plays on Simon's nickname, 'Peter,' which is roughly the English 'Rocky': Peter is 'rocky,' and on this rock Jesus would build his Church."[90]

IS THE POPE THE ANTICHRIST?

The strangest and most persistent attacks on the papacy are claims that the pope is the Antichrist or the beast from the book of Revelation. But these claims are easily rebutted.

1 John 2:22 says that the Antichrist "denies that Jesus is the Christ," but no pope has ever done this.[91] Likewise, Revelation 17 speaks of a beast that sits on seven mountains and persecutes the holy ones of God, but the Catholic Church doesn't persecute Christians and it doesn't sit on "seven mountains." Vatican City rests on Vatican Hill, which lies across the river from the seven hills of Old Rome, where Christians were crucified and fed to the lions.

Scholars agree that the "beast" in Revelation probably symbolizes a Roman emperor like Nero, or the Roman Empire as a whole because of its violent persecution of the Church during the first century.

IS THE POPE INFALLIBLE?

The doctrine of papal infallibility teaches that the pope has a special grace from God that protects him from leading Christ's Church into error. Most Protestants would admit that St. Peter was at least infallible when he wrote his first and second letters, because they're in the Bible. Catholics simply believe this kind of protection was given to Peter and each of his successors, none of whom led the Church into error.

But why should we believe the pope is infallible?

Matthew 16:18 says the "powers of death" (some translations say "gates of hell") will never prevail against the Church, so it makes sense that the pastor of Christ's Church would never steer it into hell by teaching heresy. Luke 22:31-32 records Jesus telling Peter, "Satan demanded to have you, that he might sift you like wheat, but I have prayed for you that your faith may not fail." The original Greek in the passage reveals that Satan demanded to sift "you all," or all the apostles, but Jesus prayed for "you" in the singular sense, just for Peter, that his faith would not fail.[92]

It's true that Christ once called Peter "Satan" for trying to stop the Crucifixion (Matt. 16:23). He also knew Peter would later deny him at his trial, but God doesn't call the perfect—he perfects the called. That's why Christ prayed that once Peter "turned again" from his sins, he would lead and strengthen the other apostles (Luke 22:32).

The grace of infallibility does not keep the pope from sinning (even gravely). For example, St. Paul rebuked Peter for refusing to dine with Gentiles so as not to offend his fellow Jews (Gal 2:14), but Paul didn't deny Peter's authority or show he had taught error.[93] He just reminded Peter that he needed to live up to his own teaching. As the Protestant theologian Thomas Schreiner puts it, "Peter and Paul still agreed *theologically*. Paul rebukes Peter because the latter acted *against* his convictions."[94]

Infallibility also doesn't mean the pope will have the right answer to every problem facing the Church. The gift of infallibility only keeps the pope from officially leading the Church into heresy. Some Church Fathers, such as St. Cyprian of Carthage, criticized the pope's decisions; but even Cyprian believed the pope could not lead the Church astray.

"The throne of Peter . . . from whom no error can flow."
—*St. Cyprian of Carthage, A.D. 256*[95]

PETER'S SUCCESSORS, THE BISHOPS OF ROME

Even if Peter did have infallible authority over the early Church, how do we know this authority was passed on to his successors?

In the first century, Peter's third successor, Clement, intervened in a dispute in the Church of Corinth. He warned the Corinthians they would be "in no small danger" if they disobeyed him, thus demonstrating his authority over non-Roman Christians. St. Ignatius of Antioch referred to the Roman Church as the one that teaches other churches and "presides in love" over them. In fact, the writings of Pope Clement (A.D. 92–99) and Pope Soter (A.D. 167–174) were so popular that they were read in the Church alongside Sacred Scripture.[96]

In A.D. 190, Pope Victor I excommunicated an entire region of churches for refusing to celebrate Easter on its proper date. A French bishop named St. Irenaeus thought this wasn't a good idea, but neither he nor anyone else denied that Victor had the authority to do this. Indeed, Irenaeus said of the

Church at Rome, "It is a matter of necessity that every Church should agree with this Church on account of its preeminent authority."[97] The fifth-century Council of Chalcedon read aloud a letter from Pope Leo I that defended the traditional doctrine of Christ's divinity. Once they finished, the bishops in attendance shouted, "Peter has spoken through Leo!"

Christ will always be the king of his kingdom, but like any good king, he appoints a prime minister to oversee that kingdom. Just as Israel's chief steward Eliakim was considered "a father to the inhabitants of Jerusalem and to the house of Judah" (Isa. 22:21), the bishop of Rome is a father, or pope, to those who belong to Christ's Church. He has inherited the keys to the kingdom and is faithfully charged with watching over it until the king returns in glory.

A POPE STANDS UP TO THE BARBARIANS

Popes not only protect the Church from spiritual threats, but physical ones as well. As the Roman Empire collapsed in the fourth century, barbarian hordes invaded from the north, burning villages to the ground and slaughtering people they didn't sell into slavery. The most fearsome of these barbarians was Attila the Hun, whose savage reputation for violence motivated the Romans to call him "the Scourge of God."

In A.D. 452 Attila's army gathered to attack the city of Rome, but Pope Leo I rode out to Attila, who was also on horseback. A historian who wrote about their meeting a few years later said that Attila "was so impressed by the presence of the high priest that he ordered his army to give up warfare and, after he had promised peace, he departed beyond the Danube [river]."[98]

WHY WE BELIEVE: THE POPE

- ✧ Jesus gave Peter special authority as the leader of both the apostles and the early Church.
- ✧ This authority was passed on to Peter's successors, the bishops of Rome.
- ✧ Peter and his successors enjoy the gift of infallibility, which keeps them from leading the Church into heresy.

13

Why We Have Priests

HAVE YOU EVER noticed in movies that when the heroes have to face something demonic or paranormal they almost always call in a Catholic priest to help? Even nonreligious people recognize a kind of ancient, transcendent mythos or power that radiates from a priest. But what they sense isn't a superstitious kind of magic. Rather, it's the grace of God that permanently changes a priest's soul and equips him to fight sin and even demonic forces that would attack Christ's Church.

St. Paul taught that Christ's Church would have a hierarchy composed of deacons (1 Tim. 3:8–13); presbyters, from where we get the English word "priest" (1 Tim. 5:17); and bishops (1 Tim. 3:1–7). When I first read these passages I asked myself, "Which churches today have deacons, priests, and bishops?" It must be in one of those churches, I imagined, where I would find the original church Christ established on Peter and the other apostles.

WHERE ARE PRIESTS IN THE BIBLE?

In the Old Testament, God's people had a three-tiered priesthood that has been fulfilled in Christ's Church. First, the people as a whole were called a *kingdom of priests,* because their holy conduct would allow them to intercede on behalf of an unbelieving world (Exod. 19:6). Some of them, like the Levites, were part of the *ministerial priesthood* and offered sacrifices on behalf of the people (Exod. 28:41). Finally, there was the *high priest,* who approached God's sacred dwelling among the people once a year to offer a sacrifice that made up for the peoples' sins as a whole (Exod. 28:1, Lev. 21:10).

Since the destruction of the Jerusalem Temple in A.D. 70, the Jewish sacrificial priesthood no longer exists; the Christian priesthood has now taken its place.

Just like in the Old Testament, St. Peter says every Christian belongs to *a holy priesthood* (1 Pet. 2:5), and the letter to the Hebrews says Jesus Christ is our new *high priest* (Heb. 4:14). Unlike all the other high priests, Christ was divine and without sin, so his sacrifice on the cross was able to take away the sins of the world. It is this single sacrifice that Catholic priests re-present in the form of the Eucharist (see also chapter 14). Through their service these men become the fulfillment of the *ministerial priesthood* of the Old Testament. The letter of James also refers to priests ministering to the community by offering sacraments that healed the sick and forgave sins:

> Is any among you sick? Let him call for the elders of the Church, and let them pray over him, anointing him with oil in the name of the Lord; and the prayer of faith will save the sick man, and the Lord will raise him up; and if he has committed sins, he will be forgiven. Therefore confess your sins to one another, and pray for one another, that you may be healed. The prayer of a righteous man has great power in its effects (James 5:14–16).

Today this sacrament is called the *anointing of the sick* and is also part of the *last rites*, or the prayers and sacraments given to those who are in danger of dying. One of the sacraments the priest offers, if the person is conscious and alert, is one last chance to confess his sins. Notice that James 5:16 says we ought to confess our sins "to one another," which in this context would have included the elders or priests of God's Church.

WHY DO I HAVE TO CONFESS MY SINS TO A PRIEST?

Why can't I just confess my sins directly to God? Why do I need to go to confession (or what is also called the sacrament of reconciliation)? Here's my answer: Because God loves us and has given us an amazing way to experience his forgiveness.

The Church teaches that God has given us sacraments so that we can have physical moments when we experience God's grace flooding into our hearts. Think of grace as God's free gift of life that takes away sin and makes us more and more like him. God could just give us grace in an invisible way after we say a certain prayer, but he knows we are made of matter, and matter, well, matters!

Why is it more special to get a thank-you letter in the mail than a thank-you message by email? Why is an embrace a more powerful way of saying "I love you?" It is because in these actions we experience love and gratitude with our senses as well as our mind. God understands this and that's why he gave his Church *sacraments*, or outward, physical signs of our inward reception of God's grace.

THE SEVEN SACRAMENTS

Baptism, Confirmation, the Eucharist (Lord's Supper), Penance, the Anointing of the Sick, Marriage, and Holy Orders.

There are seven sacraments, each of which has a specific way it is to be performed (the form) and a specific material that must be used (the matter). The form of baptism includes saying, "I baptize you in the name of the Father, and of the Son, and of the Holy Spirit." The matter is the water that covers the person and is the physical means by which their sins are washed away (Acts 22:16).

The sacrament of penance (confession) includes several prayers in the form, but the matter is the priest himself. His physical presence and voice is the channel through which God's grace enters the sinner's heart and reconciles him to God. St. Paul even said, "All this is from God, who through Christ reconciled us to himself and gave us the ministry of reconciliation" (2 Cor. 5:18).

A PRIEST SAVES SOULS ON THE *TITANIC*

In 1912, a British priest, Fr. Thomas Byles, booked a ticket on the *Titanic* to New York to serve at his brother's wedding. He was on the upper deck when the ship struck an iceberg and stayed behind to hear as many confessions as he could before the ship sank.

One eyewitness said, "Father Byles could have been saved, but he would not leave while one [passenger] was left . . . After I got in the boat, which was the last one to leave, and we were slowly going further away from the ship, I could hear distinctly the voice of the priest and the responses to his prayers."[99]

Fr. Byles's brother and family searched diligently for him among the survivors, but he is believed to have perished at sea; his body was never recovered. The current pastor of the church where Fr. Byles served nearly a century ago has begun the process of seeking a formal recognition of Fr. Byles's sainthood.[100]

A priest doesn't forgive sins apart from God any more than a Protestant minister who baptizes someone makes that person a Christian apart from God. A priest has the same authority to forgive sins as the apostles, to whom Jesus said, "If you forgive the sins of any, they are forgiven; if you retain the sins of any, they are retained" (John 20:23).

In order for the apostles to know a person's sins should be retained, for example, if the person wasn't actually sorry for them, they would have to know what those sins were. Barring some kind of revelation from God, this knowledge could only come from a person confessing his sins out loud. As St. Cyprian of Carthage put it in A.D. 251, "with grief and simplicity confess this very thing to God's priests, and make the conscientious avowal, put off from them the load of their minds, and seek out the salutary medicine even for slight and moderate wounds."[101]

WHY ARE PRIESTS UNMARRIED MEN?

The Catholic Church selects men to be priests because it always strives to imitate Jesus Christ. Even though many women served in Jesus' ministry, he did not call any of them to be apostles. Instead, Jesus left the Church a dogma, or an unchanging part of divine revelation, that only men can be called to stand "in the person of Christ" (Latin, *alter christus*) and serve Christ's bride the Church (Eph. 5:22–33).[102]

The requirement that priests be unmarried, or celibate, is a *discipline* rather than an unchanging *dogma*. St. Peter was married (Matt. 8:14), though we don't know if his wife was alive when he became the leader of the Church, since the Bible never mentions her.[103] Christ did not give the Church a single teaching on this question, so the Church is free to propose disciplinary rules that best serve the Body of Christ.

In the Eastern Catholic Church, married men can become priests but unmarried priests can't later get married. In the Western Church exceptions have been made for married priests who convert from other religions, like Anglicanism, but most priests are celibate.

These priests have followed a tradition given by St. Paul that says the unmarried are able to completely focus on pleasing the Lord without being hindered by the responsibility of caring for a family (1 Cor. 7:32). Paul affirmed the goodness of marriage, but he also wished that all could be celibate like him. He even described how some widows in the early Church took vows of celibacy (1 Cor. 7:7, 1 Tim. 5:12).

WHY DO CATHOLICS CALL PRIESTS "FATHER"?

If Jesus says in Matthew 23:9 to "call no man your father," then why do Catholics call priests "father"? For the same reason St. Paul called himself a father to the Christians in Corinth (1 Cor. 4:15). it is an appropriate title for the shepherds of Christ's flock.

Jesus also says in Matthew 23:8–10 to call no man teacher or "master," yet Protestants often call their seminary-educated pastors and theologians "doctor," a word that literally means "master" or "teacher."

Jesus was only warning his followers against inflating the pride of the Jewish leaders and elevating their authority above God's authority. He was not forbidding the existence of any spiritual fathers or teachers that he might call to humbly serve his Church.

Other biblical examples of living a celibate life can be seen in the prophets Elijah and Jeremiah, as well as our Lord, who said, "There are eunuchs [people incapable of sexual intercourse] who have made themselves eunuchs for the sake of the kingdom of heaven" (Matt. 19:12). *The Catholic Commentary on Holy Scripture* says that in this verse Jesus was encouraging voluntary abstinence from sexual relations, "not by self-mutilation but by self-denial."[104]

Some people say that if priests were allowed to marry there would be less sexual abuse in the Church and more men would want to be priests. But many pedophiles are married men, and being single doesn't cause someone to become attracted to children. Moreover, the priesthood isn't a job whose requirements are changed in order to attract candidates. The Bible says that when Jesus saw the crowds of people following him

> He had compassion for them, because they were harassed and helpless, like sheep without a shepherd. Then he said to his disciples, "The harvest is plentiful, but the laborers are few; pray therefore the Lord of the harvest to send out laborers into his harvest" (Matt. 9:36-38).

Priests are those men who answer God's call to go out into the world and lead lost souls back to the Good Shepherd, Jesus Christ.

WHY WE BELIEVE: PRIESTS

✧ Catholic priests are the New Covenant's fulfillment of the Old Covenant's ministerial priesthood.

- ✧ Christ only called men to be apostles, and so the Catholic priesthood only includes men.

- ✧ Traditionally, priests in the Western Church have been unmarried so they can fully imitate Christ and serve his bride, the Church.

- ✧ Catholic priests have been given authority from Christ to forgive and retain sins, which is made manifest in the sacrament of confession.

14

Why We Go to Mass

A FEW YEARS ago, some friends of ours bought a home-made-donut machine. You just poured batter into it and in one minute a bunch of mini-doughnuts rolled off its little conveyor belt. When they told their five-year-old son about it his eyes lit up and he exclaimed, "That's amazing! Now we don't have to go to Church anymore!"

Like this little boy, some people go to church for the "donuts." They might be literal donuts, but usually the "donuts" are some other nonreligious reason that gets them up earlier than usual on Sunday. They may feel the need to please a family member or spouse. Or they might go because that's just what their family always did. As they get older they might only keep that tradition going for major holidays like Easter and Christmas. But for many people, the "donuts" stop being worth it and they no longer go to Church. They might say:

> "Catholic services are boring. I don't feel like I'm getting anything out of it."
>
> "They're always asking for money."

"The music is dreadful and the homily is even worse."

When people ask me why I go to church every Sunday, I tell them it's because no matter how boring the homily, no matter how terrible the music, no matter what else is happening, the bread and wine on the altar at every Catholic Mass becomes the body and blood of our savior Jesus Christ. I go because that bread and wine don't just symbolize Jesus; they actually become his body, blood, soul, and divinity. Jesus is there, not just every Sunday, but every day, ready to be received by the faithful so they can have eternal life.

THE NEW PASSOVER

The first time I visited a Catholic Church, the person who invited me explained that the services are called "Mass" because the name comes from the Latin word *missa,* which means "to send forth." Catholics attend Mass so they can be equipped and "sent forth" to share the gospel with the entire world. When that friend told me about the "sacrifice of the Mass," however, I stopped a few feet from the church entrance.

"Sacrifice? You're not going to kill a goat up there on the altar, are you? Because I'm not sure I'm ready for that."

He laughed and said that the sacrifice would be the bread and wine brought up to the altar, called the Eucharist, which comes from a Greek word that means "thanksgiving." The *Catechism* says, "For in the blessed Eucharist is contained the whole spiritual good of the Church, namely Christ himself, our Pasch" (CCC 1324).

Pasch means "Passover" and is a reference to an event the Jewish people still celebrate. When they were enslaved in Egypt, God told his people to kill a lamb that was without blemish or defect so that the angel of death that was sent to punish the Egyptians would "pass over" their homes (Exod. 12:43-51). Christians also have a lamb who was sacrificed so that spiritual death would pass over them: Jesus Christ.

John the Baptist said that Jesus was "the lamb of God, who takes away the sin of the world" (John 1:29), and St. Paul said, "Christ, our Paschal Lamb, has been sacrificed" (1 Cor. 5:7). The Passover lamb in the Old Testament had to be a male, without blemish, and his legs could not be broken (Exod. 12:5,46). Christ, our Passover lamb, is male, without sin (Heb. 4:15), and during the Crucifixion his legs were not broken (John 19:33). Finally, the Passover was not complete until the lamb was eaten, and so the "Passover" that Christians still celebrate must be completed in the same way.

FOOD INDEED, DRINK INDEED

Since Jesus did not want us to be cannibals, he gave us his body and blood to consume under the miraculous form of bread and wine. He said:

> Truly, truly, I say to you, unless you eat the flesh of the Son of man and drink his blood, you have no life in you; he who eats my flesh and drinks my blood has eternal life, and I will raise him up at the last day. For my flesh is food indeed, and my blood is drink indeed. He who eats my flesh and drinks my blood abides in me, and I in him. As the living Father sent me, and I live because of the Father, so he who eats me will live because of me (John 6:53-57).

The original Greek in this passage communicates an even more powerful message than what we read in English. Earlier in John 6, Jesus uses *phago*, a generic word for eating, but in these verses he switches to *trogo,* which means "to gnaw or chew." Likewise, Jesus uses the word *sarx*, which refers to the soft, fleshy substance that covers our bones, and not *soma,* which just means "body." Jesus' word choice, as rendered in the Greek, shows that he is talking about real, physical chewing and eating of his very flesh.

> **"My flesh is food indeed, and my blood is drink indeed."**
> *—John 6:55*

After his resurrection, Jesus appeared to two of his followers on a road to the city of Emmaus. He hid his identity from them until after he blessed and broke bread for them to eat. Jesus made it clear that after his resurrection all of his disciples would not see him in a human form, but that he would instead be "known to them in the breaking of the bread" (Luke 24:35).

When I told one of my non-Catholic friends that I went to Mass he scoffed. "Don't you think it's weird that Catholics believe they're eating Jesus' actual flesh and blood?" I then showed him John 6:53-57 and asked him what he thought Jesus meant when he said, "He who eats my flesh and drinks my blood has eternal life." My friend read the passage, closed the Bible, and while shrugging his shoulders said, "It's just a metaphor."

But that explanation didn't sit well with me.

It's true Jesus used metaphors to describe his mission. He said of himself, "I am the door" (John 10:9) and "I am the vine" (John 15:5), but in those cases Jesus didn't also tell us to "oil his *true* hinges" or "water his *true* roots." In addition, no one rejected Jesus for using metaphors involving the door or the vine, but when Jesus said that a person must eat his flesh to have eternal life, the Bible tells us that "many of his disciples drew back and no longer walked with him" (John 6:66).[105]

THE FIRST CHRISTIANS BELIEVED IN THE REAL PRESENCE

St. Paul told the Corinthians that whoever "eats the bread or drinks the cup of the Lord in an unworthy manner will be guilty of profaning the body and blood of the Lord" (1 Cor. 11:27). Just sixty years later, St. Ignatius of Antioch said, "The Eucharist is the flesh of our Savior Jesus Christ, flesh which suffered for our sins and which the Father, in his goodness, raised up again."[106] J.N.D. Kelly admits that in the early Church, "the consecrated bread and wine were taken to be, and were treated and designated as, the Savior's body and blood."[107]

IT STILL LOOKS LIKE BREAD AND WINE!

At the Last Supper before his Crucifixion, Jesus offered the disciples bread and wine. Jesus did not say, "This bread *contains* my body" or "I am *in* this wine." Jesus simply said of the bread, "Take, eat; this is my body" and of the wine "Drink of it, all of you; for this is my blood of the covenant" (Matt 26:26–28). The Church teaches that when they are consecrated at Mass, the substance of these things changes into the body and blood of Christ although the appearances of the bread and wine remain.

A substance is the "metaphysical core" of an object that unites all of an object's appearances into a single entity. For example, humans look very different as they grow from being infants and become adults. In fact, many of our cells die and are replaced by new cells, but through all these changes we remain the same person. That's because we possess an invisible, underlying *substance,* or a metaphysical core that unites our parts. This unity is only broken at death, when the soul leaves the body and we begin to decompose.

At Mass the bread and wine do not *transform* into the body and blood of Christ, because their form, or how the bread and wine look and taste to us, does not change. Rather, the *substance* of the bread and wine changes into the substance of the body and blood of Christ.

Through this miracle, God causes the appearances of bread and wine to remain but replaces the underlying reality that unites these appearances, the substance, with the body and blood of Christ. That's why Catholics teach that during the Consecration at Mass the bread and wine *transubstantiate,* or change in substance, into the body and blood of Christ. This explains how we can consume what appear to be bread and wine and still be faithful to Jesus' command to "eat his flesh and drink his blood."[108]

Finally, at Mass Christ is not re-sacrificed on the cross. Unlike the animal sacrifices of the Old Testament, Christ's sacrifice was perfect and does not need to be repeated on a continual basis (Heb. 10:10). Instead, at every Mass Christ's sacrifice is *re-presented*, or made present again, to the Father, and we receive the saving effects of his sacrifice by consuming it under the form of bread and wine in the Eucharist.[109] The *Didache,* a first-century catechism manual, even tells Christians to "assemble on the Lord's day, and break bread and offer the Eucharist; but first make confession of your faults, so that your sacrifice may be a pure one."[110]

FALL AT HIS FEET

After I became Catholic I used to count the number of times I'd received the Lord in the Eucharist. "My seventh time receiving Jesus!" I'd say to myself. By now I've lost count how many times I've received the Eucharist, and when I'm tired and bored at Mass I become tempted to just "get through it."

Then I remember a story the philosopher Peter Kreeft likes to tell. He says that when one of his students explained the Eucharist to a Muslim friend, the man said, "I don't think you really do believe that." The student asked why he thought that and his Muslim friend said, "If I believed that thing that looks like a little round piece of bread was really Allah [God] Himself, I think I would just faint. I would fall at His feet like a dead man."[111]

I'm glad what I "get out of" Mass isn't just a warm, fuzzy feeling. I'd rather have the feeling of receiving the God of the universe in my hands, on my lips, and into my very body. I'd rather have the joy of knowing that God has humbled himself to become a physical object that makes the temple of my body (1 Cor. 6:19) home to his actual presence. In that way, Jesus' very life is joined with mine so I can share eternal life with him.

HE GAVE HIS LIFE FOR THE EUCHARIST

In the third century, a young Roman boy named Tarcisius who assisted at Mass was asked to bring the Eucharist to Christians who were dying in prison. It was illegal to practice the Faith, so Christians hid in underground tombs called catacombs. When Tarcisius emerged from the catacombs, a group of non-Christians demanded he hand over the Eucharist. He refused and so they beat him with clubs until he died. According to the Church's records of those who were martyred for the Faith, "they could find no trace of Christ's Sacrament either in his hands or in his clothing. The Christians took up the body of the martyr and buried it with honor in the cemetery of Callistus."[112]

WHY WE BELIEVE: MASS AND THE EUCHARIST

- Jesus is the new Passover lamb who was sacrificed to take away the sins of the world.

- The Passover lamb had to be eaten, which is why Jesus gave us his flesh and blood under the form of bread and wine.

- Christ is not sacrificed again at Mass. Rather, his one sacrifice on the cross is re-presented to the Father and through it we receive God's grace.

15

Why We
Baptize Babies

I STILL REMEMBER the night I was baptized. When my name was called I walked up to the front of the church and dipped my feet into the cool water of the baptismal font. As the water swirled around my ankles, I lifted up my palms and closed my eyes.

I don't remember thinking about anything except the priest's voice saying, "I baptize you in the name of the Father . . ." As he poured the water over my head I opened my eyes to see what looked like a shimmering curtain separating me from the rest of the church. He continued, " . . . and of the Son, and of the Holy Spirit."

I wiped the water from my eyes and saw hundreds of people breaking out into thunderous applause, including my non-Catholic parents. As I stepped out of the font I thought of the conversion of St. Paul, who had become a hero of mine as I prepared to be received into the Church.

According to the Bible, after he met the risen Jesus, St. Paul was left blind until God's messenger Ananias visited him. He told Paul, "The God of our fathers appointed you to know his will . . . you will be a witness for him to all men of what you have seen and heard. And now why do you wait? Rise and be baptized, and wash away your sins, calling on his name" (Acts 22:14–16).

HOW BAPTISM WORKS

Jesus didn't say baptism merely showed other people we were Christians. Instead, Jesus declared that, "Unless one is born of water and the Spirit, he cannot enter the kingdom of God" (John 3:5). St. Peter told a crowd in Jerusalem, "Repent, and be baptized every one of you . . . for the forgiveness of your sins" (Acts 2:38), and in his own letter to the entire Church Peter said that "baptism . . . now saves you" (1 Pet. 3:21).

Before Jesus' earthly ministry, a prophet named John the Baptist called people to give up their sins and faithfully worship the one, true God. John's baptism didn't take away sin, but rather showed that a person was sorry for his sins.[113] However, John did say that, while he baptized with water, someone coming after him who was greater than him (or Jesus) would baptize with the Holy Spirit and with fire (Matt. 3:11). Jesus' baptism didn't just symbolize a person rejecting his sins; it actually took away that person's sins.

BAPTIZED WITH FIRE?

In the Bible, fire often symbolizes purification, such as when God's way of making us holy is compared to how a blacksmith uses fire to burn away the corrupt parts of a metal. Just as the blacksmith's fire leaves only pure, stainless metal, the fire of God's love leaves a pure believer who is free from the stain of sin (Prov. 17:3, Sir. 2:4-6). The Bible says that God is a consuming fire (Heb. 12:29), which means God is able to purify and "burn away" our sin so that we can stand sinless before him at the final judgment (1 Cor. 3:15).

God knows that we comprehend the world by thinking *and* by feeling. In order to help us truly understand that he cleanses us from our sins, God chose an instrument that every culture on earth associates with life and health—water. That's why Jesus instructed the disciples to baptize all nations in the name of the Father, Son and Holy Spirit (Matt. 28:19).

PERSONAL VERSUS ORIGINAL SIN

I had been baptized as a young adult, which means that every sin I committed before that point was forgiven. But if baptism washes away sin, and babies don't commit any sins, then why do Catholics bother to baptize babies? The reason is that along with personal sin, or acts of wrongdoing that violate God's law, there is another kind of sin we all have—original sin.

WHAT IS SIN?

- **Original sin**: An inherited absence of God's grace that inclines us to sin and suffer death (CCC 403-404).
- **Personal sin**: Choosing to do evil that violates God's eternal law, or failing to do good (CCC 1849-1850).

Unlike personal sin, original sin is not an evil thing we've done but an absence of God's grace in our souls. Baptism "removes" original sin by filling our souls with the love and life of God, or grace. So, when I was baptized, not only did God forgive every sin I committed, but he filled my heart with his life and took away the stain of original sin. In that moment he gave me, as Paul says, "the spirit of sonship. When we cry, 'Abba! [literally, Daddy!] Father!' it is the Spirit himself bearing witness with our spirit that we are children of God" (Rom. 8:15-16).

The reason this absence of grace is called *original sin* is because it is a consequence of the very first sin humans committed. When our first parents, Adam and Eve, disobeyed God, they lost the gift of God's favor that protected them from death and suffering. After losing this grace they could not pass it down to their descendants, who in turn could not pass it down to us. Adam and Eve's disobedience corrupted our human nature and made it possible for humans to suffer and die. Baptism cannot prevent our physical deaths, because it does not change our physical natures. However, it does change our spiritual nature, so through baptism we are saved from spiritual death by being united to Jesus Christ.

THE FATAL FALL

Some people say it's not fair for God to punish us because of something Adam and Eve did, but original sin is not a *punishment*. Instead, it is a *consequence* of what Adam and Eve did that we have to endure.[114]

To understand this, imagine a man is given an inheritance that makes him rich, but in his greed he steals more money from the estate of his deceased relative. The man's wife and children, who didn't know he did this, are thrilled about never having to worry about money again—until the police arrive, arrest the man, and the courts take back all the money he inherited.

The courts don't punish the man's family because they did nothing wrong. However, the man's family still suffers because they would have been blessed with riches if he had not stolen more money. In the same way, we would have enjoyed supernatural gifts of grace if Adam and Eve had not fallen from grace and rebelled against God. St. Paul says that because of the fall of man, "sin came into the world through one man and death through sin, and so death spread to all men because all men sinned" (Rom. 5:12).

> "O truly necessary sin of Adam,
> destroyed completely by the Death of Christ!
> O happy fault
> that earned so great, so glorious a Redeemer!"
> *—Exultet, sung every year at the Church's Easter Vigil*

Even though one man's disobedience cursed humanity, one man's obedience saved it (Rom. 5:19). St. Paul says that Christ's sacrifice atoned or made up not just for Adam's sin, but for the sins of the whole world (1 John 2:2). He also says that we are freed from sin by dying and rising with Christ, but how exactly do we "die and rise" with Christ? St. Paul explains:

> Do you not know that all of us who have been baptized into Christ Jesus were baptized into his death? We were buried therefore with him by baptism into death, so that as Christ was raised from the dead by the glory of the Father, we too might walk in newness of life (Romans 6:3-4).

BRINGING CHILDREN TO CHRIST

The Bible says baptism washes away sin (Acts 22:16) and makes us members of the Body of Christ (1 Cor. 12:13). Should we exclude babies from the Body of Christ just because they can't choose to be baptized? Of course not! Babies never chose to be afflicted with original sin either, but we can choose to deliver them from this condition through baptism. Jesus even said, "Let the children come to me, and do not hinder them; for to such belongs the kingdom of heaven" (Matt. 19:14).

It's true the Bible never explicitly describes babies being baptized, but it does describe entire households being baptized, which may have included young children (Acts 16:15, 16:33; 1 Cor. 1:16). Although the Bible never describes the way we should baptize someone, that doesn't stop us from baptizing people.

Should we pour water over a person's head? Should we fully immerse him in water? Could we just sprinkle water on people, especially if they live in places like the desert, which barely have any water? God's written word doesn't tell us, but God's spoken word, preserved in Sacred Tradition, does. The *Didache* records how the first-century Church practiced baptism:

> Concerning baptism, baptize in this manner: Having said all these things beforehand, baptize in the name of the Father and of the Son and of the Holy Spirit in living water [that is, in running water, as in a river]. If there is no living water, baptize in other water; and, if you are not able to use cold water, use warm. If you have neither, pour water three times upon the head in the name of the Father, Son, and Holy Spirit.[115]

The Bible also teaches that the New Covenant in Christ is greater than the Old Covenant God had with Israel (Heb. 8:6). Since the Old Covenant included babies through circumcision (Gen. 17:12), this means the New Covenant must also include babies or else it would be inferior to the Old Covenant. In fact, St. Paul calls baptism "the circumcision of Christ" (Col. 2:11).

Some people in the early Church believed this meant that parents must wait eight days to baptize their children, because that's how long people waited to circumcise babies in the Old

Covenant. But the Fathers of the Church said babies should be baptized as soon as possible, especially since children in that time were at risk of dying soon after birth.

"NO ONE IS HELD BACK"

In the third century, St. Cyprian said, "The mercy and grace of God ought to be denied to no man born . . . no one is held back from baptism and grace, how much more, then, should an infant not be held back."[116]

Denying babies God's grace through baptism so that they can choose it later as an adult would be like denying a baby medicine so that he can choose to take it "for himself" when he gets older. Sin is just too serious to leave in anyone's body, especially a child's. That's why even though I was baptized as an adult, I give all my children shortly after they're born a gift I wasn't blessed with at their age—the grace of God poured into their hearts through the sacrament of baptism.

WHY WE BELIEVE: BAPTISM

✧ Baptism takes away sin, unites us with Christ, and makes us members of his body, the Church.

✧ Infants must be baptized because they are born with original sin. Baptism is the ordinary means by which God removes original sin and makes us his adopted children.

✧ The early Church only debated when infants should be baptized, not if they should be baptized.

PART 4

SAINTS & SINNERS

16

Why We Believe in Spite of Scandal

SHORTLY AFTER I became Catholic, I visited a party with some of my nonreligious friends, who were watching news coverage about the clergy sex abuse scandal. It seems that in several large dioceses priests who had been accused of abusing children weren't reported to the police. They were instead transferred to other parishes (or churches), putting untold numbers of children at risk.

As I entered the room, one of my friends turned to me, smirked, and said, "Great job picking a new religion, Trent."

PUTTING SCANDAL INTO PERSPECTIVE

It feels like a punch to the gut when something or someone you care about is caught up in scandal. You may even be tempted to cut off all association with a scandalized group or person and try to make a fresh start. But as St. Augustine is reported to have said, "The Church is not a hotel for saints, it is a hospital for sinners." The issue is not whether the patients are sinners, or even if the staff are sinners. The issue is whether the hospital (or the Church) has the *cure* for sin that has infected everyone. Pope Paul VI put it this way:

> The Church is therefore holy, though having sinners in her midst, because she herself has no other life but the life of grace. If they live her life, her members are sanctified [or made holy]; if they move away from her life, they fall into sins and disorders that prevent the radiation of her sanctity.[117]

The clergy abuse scandal does not prove there is no God or that Christ did not establish the Catholic Church. If anything, the revulsion we have against child abuse shows that some acts are always wrong—no matter what. Since universal moral laws must come from a universal moral lawgiver, or God, this means the clergy abuse scandal should push someone *away* from atheism, not toward it.

The scandal also doesn't justify leaving Catholicism for a Protestant church, since sex abuse is not only a "Catholic" problem. According to the John Jay College of Criminal Justice, about 4 percent of priests who served between 1950 and 2002 have been accused of sexual abuse (note that accusations do not always mean a crime was committed).[118] Insurance company premiums suggest that similar rates of abuse exist in Protestant churches. According to one insurance industry spokeswoman, "Our claims experience shows this happens evenly across denominations."[119]

This does not excuse incidents of sex abuse in the Church, but it does help us respond to those incidents. Just as we wouldn't say public schools are "full of pedophile teachers," we shouldn't slander or abandon the Church because of the sinful actions of a tiny minority of the clergy.

IS ABUSE JUST A CATHOLIC PROBLEM?

Ernie Allen, the director of the National Center for Missing and Exploited Children, said in an interview with *Newsweek* magazine, "We don't see the Catholic Church as a hotbed of this or a place that has a bigger problem than anyone else. I can tell you without hesitation that we have seen cases in many religious settings, from traveling evangelists to mainstream ministers to rabbis and others."[120]

GETTING THE FACTS RIGHT

Most accusations of sexual abuse among priests come from incidents that took place between 1950 and 1980. At that time it was thought that the urge to commit sexual abuse could be treated with therapy, and so involving law enforcement was not always necessary. According to Dr. Monica Applewhite, who has spent more than twenty years studying abuse and how to prevent it, "These treatment-based interventions for sexual criminals [instead of incarceration] were not only enormously prevalent in the United States, but surveys of ordinary citizens showed that they were enormously popular."[121]

Modern psychology has now shown, however, that sex offenders are very likely to commit more crimes in the future. That's why the Catholic Church has taken steps to increase transparency and accountability in the area of reporting sexual abuse. The Church has created offices of safe environment and child protection that have trained millions of adults to recognize signs of abuse. Dioceses across the world have instituted zero tolerance policies that require immediate and mandatory reporting of alleged abuse to law enforcement. In

2015, Pope Francis created a special tribunal for disciplining bishops who had been negligent in their response to allegations of abuse.[122]

According to journalist David Gibson, "The Catholic Church may be the safest place for children. Whatever its past record, the Catholic Church in the U.S. has made unparalleled strides in educating their flock about child sexual abuse and ensuring that children are safe in Catholic environments."[123]

HISTORY FULL OF SCANDALS?

The clergy abuse scandal isn't the only event in Church history that has been misunderstood. Consider the Crusades, which were not cases of the Church trying to forcibly convert people or steal their land. According to Thomas Madden, one of the world's leading experts on the subject, "The crusades remain today one of the most commonly misunderstood events in Western history."[124]

Instead of seeking riches and conquest, the Crusaders risked life and limb to rescue Christians whose land and homes had been overrun by Muslim invaders. Even Christian pilgrims who visited the region risked their lives to worship in the Holy Land. For example, thirty years before the First Crusade, a group of 7,000 peaceful German pilgrims were viciously massacred.[125] This, among other events, prompted Pope Urban II to call the First Crusade. In a speech he gave in 1095 the pope said:

> Let those who for a long time have been robbers now become knights. Let those who have been fighting against their brothers and relatives now fight in a proper way against the barbarians. Let those who have been serving as mercenaries for small pay now obtain the eternal reward.[126]

This does not mean the Crusaders were always virtuous. Some of them took advantage of "the fog of war" and committed unspeakable atrocities against civilians and even other Crusaders. But this does not make the Crusades an unjust war any more than the firebombing of the city of Dresden, which killed thousands of German civilians, and made the Allies unjust aggressors during World War II.

A RABBI DEFENDS THE POPE

Another historical myth about the Church involves Pope Pius XII allegedly ignoring or even actively helping the Nazis. However, that claim originally came from a 1963 Soviet propaganda play called *The Deputy*. According to Rabbi David Dalin, author of the book *The Myth of Hitler's Pope*:

> "Eugenio Pacelli [the future Pope Pius XII] was one of Hitler's earliest and most consistent critics and . . . as both the Vatican Secretary of State and subsequently as pope, was in fact a friend of the Jewish people who was instrumental in rescuing and sheltering a great many Jews from the clutches of the Nazis."[127]

Finally, when people focus only on scandal they forget how the Catholic Church has been a force for good in the world. The Church built the Western world's first universities, hospitals, orphanages, and homes for the dying. Its missionaries preached the gospel in far-off lands, where they had to fight barbaric practices like wife-burning, foot-binding, and child marriages. In the fourth century, the Roman emperor complained that Christians "support not only their own poor but ours as well, all men see that our people lack aid from us."[128]

In his history of medicine, historian Roy Porter says, "Christianity planted the hospital" and it was considered a mark of holiness to expose oneself to infection in order to care for the sick.[129] This legacy continues today in the Catholic Church, which is the largest provider of nongovernmental health care in the entire world.[130]

A PRIEST BRINGS LEPERS TO CHRIST

Throughout human history many victims of leprosy (a disease that causes numbness in the limbs and skin lesions) were banished to "leper colonies."[131] One large colony existed on the island of Molokai in Hawaii where, in 1873, a man named Fr. Damien volunteered to be the colony's first priest.

For the next eleven years Fr. Damien did what many weakened lepers could not: he built homes, churches, and public utilities. He healed the sick, cared for orphans and widows, and celebrated the sacraments. In 1884 he contracted leprosy and five years later was buried beneath the same tree he slept under when he first arrived on the island.

In 2009 the Church declared him to be St. Damien of Molokai. His life could be summarized in these words he shared with one of his friends: "I make myself a leper with the lepers to gain all to Jesus Christ."[132]

RESPONDING TO "SPIRITUAL MALPRACTICE"

After one of my public presentations, a woman approached me and asked, "How can Catholics have the true Church when their priests do such awful things?" I asked in reply, "Are you saying that all priests abuse children?"

"Oh, of course not," she insisted, "but too many of them have."

"What percent is too many for you? Personally I think one

is too many, but does that prove the Catholic faith isn't true?

"If they're really men of God in Christ's Church," she asked, "then how could they do that?"

I responded, "Let me ask you, does the devil hate Christ's Church?"

"Absolutely!"

"Then of all the members of the Church, who is he going to attack the most?"

She thought for a moment and then said, "The priests!"

This is why we must pray for priests as well as for everyone else who fights against sin and despair in our world. This does not mean that we should excuse or ignore sins that any Catholic commits, even if that person is a priest. If you or someone you love was hurt by a member of the Catholic Church, know that I am sorry. Those responsible for these crimes, no matter who they are, must be brought to justice. Even if it turned out the pope was guilty of abusing a child I would wholeheartedly say he needed to be imprisoned. But just as a victim of abuse should not be blamed for a crime committed against him, the Church as a whole should not be blamed for crimes committed by priests or other Catholics who violate its teachings.

Leaving the Church because a priest or layperson committed a serious sin would be like swearing off hospitals because a doctor committed malpractice. What that doctor did was wrong, but that doesn't change the fact that the hospital is still the best place to go if you're sick. Similarly, Christ gave his Church the means to free us from sin, so we do ourselves no favors if we reject that remedy because some Catholics who fell into scandal refused to take it.

WHY WE BELIEVE: OVERCOMING SCANDAL

- ✧ Jesus never promised that his Church would be free of sinners, only that it would provide the means to save sinners.
- ✧ Some particular allegations of scandal are built on lies or misrepresentations of Church history.
- ✧ Scandal should not be ignored, but it also shouldn't be used as a reason to leave the Church, because the sins of a few do not disprove the truth of what the Church as a whole teaches.

17

Why We Believe that Faith Works Through Love

ONCE WHEN I was eating in a cafeteria I noticed two girls at another table smiling at me. I smiled back and they walked over to where I was sitting as I thought to myself, "Still got it . . ." One of them then said to me, "Hi, could I ask you a question?"

"Sure," I said, in as relaxed a tone as possible.

"Would you mind answering a few survey questions for us?"

"Guess I don't got it," I thought to myself.

They first asked me what religion I was and I told them I was Catholic. One of the girls then asked me, "On a scale from one to ten how confident are you that you're going to heaven?"

I though for a moment and replied, "I'm pretty sure I'm going to heaven, but I can't give it a number . . ." The second girl jumped in and said, "Actually the correct number is ten (I didn't know you could get a survey question wrong!). All you need to do to go to heaven is believe in Jesus Christ. If you do that you can never lose your salvation."

While this sounds wonderful, the problem with this view of salvation is that it is unbiblical. The Bible does not teach that simply making an act of faith guarantees heaven for us. Instead, it teaches that salvation is a process of "faith working through love" (Gal. 5:6), made possible through our spiritual adoption into God's family.

GOD'S PLAN OF SALVATION

God desires the salvation of all people (1 Tim. 2:4). That's why in one act of love Jesus Christ, who is fully man, represented all of us on the cross and perfectly obeyed God's law in a way no other human could. Because Jesus is fully divine, his death on the cross had infinite value. It was a sacrifice of love that was so good it made up not just for the sins of Christians, but the sins of the entire world (1 John 2:2).

Does that mean everyone will go to heaven?

God has given everyone enough grace to come to know him and his offer of salvation. But since God is love, and love never forces itself on the beloved, God will not force people to be saved. Some people will reject God's offer of salvation, but other people will not resist God's grace. They will see the ugliness of sin and ask God to help them escape it. They will follow the Bible's three-step plan for being saved:

- *Repent* (turn away from sin)
- *Believe* (turn toward Christ)
- *Receive* (be united to Christ)

In his first sermon, St. Peter told a crowd in Jerusalem, "Repent, and be baptized every one of you in the name of

Jesus Christ for the forgiveness of your sins; and you shall receive the gift of the Holy Spirit" (Acts 2:38). St. Paul likewise told the Philippian jailer, "Believe in the Lord Jesus, and you will be saved, you and your household" (Acts 16:31). The text goes on to say that the jailer "was baptized at once, with all his family" (Acts 16:33).

The apostles preached that adult converts (like me) had to repent of sin, believe in Jesus, and then receive Jesus by being baptized. However, the order of these steps can be changed. For someone who hasn't committed a personal sin yet, like a baby, it would look like this:

✧ *Receive* (be united to Christ)

✧ *Repent* (turn away from sin)

✧ *Believe* (turn toward Christ)

When my wife was a baby she (like most Catholics) was baptized. This removed the stain of original sin and filled her soul with God's grace. This grace helped her when she learned about Jesus, and gave her "spiritual motivation" to repent from sin and believe in Christ and his Church.

SALVATION: PAST, PRESENT, AND FUTURE

So is that all there is to our salvation? Repent, believe, and receive? That's all there is to our *initial salvation*, or our being adopted into God's family. Our final salvation isn't complete until we enter into heaven. Between the beginning and end of salvation are all the moments we live out in this life where we remember Jesus' teaching that "he who endures to the end will be saved" (Matt. 10:22).

Salvation does not consist of a single moment when we accept Christ. Rather, it is a process through which we live out our faith and obey Christ until death. Here's a scenario that illustrates what I mean.

Imagine you are caught in a storm at sea with some friends and your boat is sinking. You hear a broadcast on your radio telling you that if you want to be saved you must put on life jackets, report your position, and wait for help to arrive. As the boat pitches up and down and water sprays over the bow, you reply into the radio, "Yes, save us!" You then put on the life jackets and dive into the water.

Two days go by and your rescuers are nowhere to be seen. One of your friends says help isn't coming and decides to swim to shore on his own: he is never seen again. A few days later a rescue boat finds you, pulls you onto the deck, and you breathe a sigh of relief. "Saved!"

But when exactly were you saved? Was it when you set foot on the rescue boat? Or was it when you made the initial radio call? The Bible teaches that salvation is a process that begins in the *past* through faith, continues throughout our lives in the *present*, and ends with our *future* eternal glory in heaven. Let's take a look at each part of our salvation:

Past Salvation: Ephesians 2:8-9 says, "By grace you have been saved through faith; and this is not your own doing, it is the gift of God—not because of works, lest any man should boast." That's true! Whether it was my wife who was baptized as a baby and later came to believe in Christ, or myself who came to believe in Christ and chose to be baptized, both of us were saved by *faith*. God adopted us as his children and we did nothing to earn that gift of faith; we simply chose not to reject it. This is similar to how the people on the sinking ship did not reject the rescue offer they heard on the radio, but accepted it and waited for help.

When the Bible says we are not saved by works, it means we did nothing to earn the first moment of our salvation. But as we will see, works do play a role in the process of our salvation.

JUSTIFIED BY FAITH ALONE?

In Romans 3:28 Paul says, "We hold that a man is justified by faith apart from works of law." The Reformers took this to mean that Paul condemned the idea that good works have any part in our salvation. But Protestant scholars like James Dunn and N.T. Wright have shown that Reformers like Luther and Calvin misunderstood Paul's argument.[133]

When Paul talked about being justified, or being made righteous apart from the Law, he didn't mean good works have nothing to do with our salvation. What he meant was that a person is saved apart from obeying the Law of Moses, or that people don't have to become Jews before they can become Christians.

That's why in the very next verse Paul says, "Or is God the God of Jews only? Is he not the God of Gentiles also?" (Rom. 3:29). It's also why in Galatians 5:6 Paul says, "For in Christ Jesus neither circumcision nor uncircumcision is of any avail, but faith working through love."

Paul did not teach that works have nothing to do with our salvation, because he said that God "will render to every man according to his works: to those who by patience in well-doing seek for glory and honor and immortality, he will give eternal life" (Rom 2:6-7).

Present Salvation: In Philippians 2:12 Paul tells us, "Work out your own salvation with fear and trembling." As long as a person remains in a state of grace, he will go to heaven after death. John 3:36 says, "He who believes in the Son has eternal life; he who does not *obey the Son* [emphasis added] shall not see life." That's why James 2:24 says, "A person is justified by works and not by faith alone."

There are no specific works that "earn" our salvation. Instead, we merit salvation by cooperating with God's grace to do the works he prepared for us before we were even born (Eph. 2:10). Because we are God's adopted children, everything we do in Christ, even mundane, day-to-day tasks, pleases God when they are done in a spirit of humility and charity. However, if we commit a mortal sin (1 John 5:17), and fall from grace (Gal. 5:4), then we risk losing our salvation (Heb. 10:28-29).

If we give up our faith or commit a serious sin and separate ourselves from God, then we will be like the foolish shipwreck survivor who tried to swim to shore on his own and perished. In fact, St. Paul warned his disciple Timothy not to be like people who rejected what their conscience told them and "made shipwreck of their faith" (1 Tim 1:19).

Future Salvation: Just as the shipwreck survivors' ordeal wasn't over until they made it to dry land, our salvation is not complete until we enter into God's kingdom. But in Romans 10:13 Paul says, "Everyone who calls upon the name of the Lord will be saved." Doesn't that mean all we have to do is believe and we know we will be saved?

Paul does not mean a person's salvation is finished immediately after he believes in Jesus. In Romans 13:11, Paul says of those who had believed for a while, "Salvation is nearer to us now than when we first believed." Faith begins our salvation, and if we "kept the faith" (2 Tim. 4:7) *then* we "will be saved." That's why Paul warns the Church at Rome that if they don't continue in God's kindness, "you too will be cut off" (Rom. 11:22).

Fortunately for us, God has given his Church the "ministry of reconciliation." Anyone who separates himself from Christ, no matter what he or she has done, can be restored to an intimate relationship with God through the sacrament of confession (John 20:23). Those who choose reconciliation with God know that "any one [who] is in Christ, he is a new creation; the old has passed away, behold, the new has come" (2 Cor. 5:17–18).

FAITH THAT WORKS IN LOVE

Through God's grace our hearts are transformed so we can perform works of love that please him and prepare us to enter into his kingdom. The effect of this grace can be seen in people like Mother Teresa (now St. Teresa of Calcutta), who devoted her life to serving the poor and the dying. She founded the Missionaries of Charity, which now has thousands of members who take a vow to give "wholehearted free service to the poorest of the poor."

Part of that service includes homes for dying people who could not be helped in hospitals and whose families have abandoned them. The missionaries founded the first home for people dying specifically of HIV/AIDS in New York's Greenwich Village in 1985. A similar home was opened in Washington, D.C., despite public protests from residents who did not want "those kinds of people" in their neighborhood.[134]

Mother Teresa summarized her work and her faith in this way: "By blood, I am Albanian. By citizenship, an Indian. By faith, I am a Catholic nun. As to my calling, I belong to the world. As to my heart, I belong entirely to the Heart of Jesus."[135]

WHY WE BELIEVE: FAITH WORKING THROUGH LOVE

- We are initially saved in the past through the gift of faith that comes from God and motivates us to be baptized (or motivates someone to baptize us when we are infants).

- We are saved in the present by obeying God and working out our salvation (Phil. 2:13) so that we can receive our final salvation in the future.

- Salvation involves being united to Christ and adopted into God's family, where God freely rewards his children for the good works they do with the gift of grace (James 2:24, Rom. 2:6–8).

18

Why We Believe in Purgatory

C.S. LEWIS, THE author of *Mere Christianity* and *The Chronicles of Narnia*, was not Catholic but he did believe in the existence of purgatory. He knew dying does not change our sinful hearts, so God must do something to us after death in order to make us fit to spend eternal life with him. Lewis said, "Our souls *demand* Purgatory, don't they?[136]

1 John 5:17 says, "All wrongdoing is sin, but there is sin which is not mortal." The Church refers to *mortal* sins as our freely chosen, gravely evil acts that destroy God's love in our hearts. These sins forfeit our hope of eternal life with God unless we ask God to forgive them through the sacrament of reconciliation (confession).[137]

Unlike mortal sins, *venial* sins hurt the soul but do not kill God's grace within it. These are sins that people commit in their day-to-day life that do not completely separate them from God but do hurt their relationship with him. Catholics don't have to confess these sins to a priest (but they can if they wish), and the Eucharist also cleanses us of these sins. But what happens to people who don't seek the sacraments and die in an unclean state of venial sin?

C.S. LEWIS DESCRIBES THE NEED FOR PURGATORY

Would it not break the heart if God said to us, "It is true, my son, that your breath smells and your rags drip with mud and slime, but we are charitable here and no one will upbraid you with these things, nor draw away from you. Enter into the joy"? Should we not reply, "With submission, sir, and if there is no objection, I'd rather be cleaned first."

"It may hurt, you know."

"Even so, sir."

Since these people died in a state of grace and friendship with God, there is no possibility they will go to hell. But Revelation 21:27 says that nothing unclean will be in heaven. It logically follows, therefore, that these saved souls will be purged of their sins prior to spending eternity with God. According to the *Catechism*, "The Church gives the name purgatory to this final purification of the elect, which is entirely different from the punishment of the damned" (CCC 1031).

Purgatory is not an alternative to heaven and hell nor is it a "second chance" to choose God. All souls that go to purgatory belong to people who died in God's friendship. Purgatory isn't a place as much as it is a state of existence after death, where we will be purified from sin. C.S. Lewis understood that because God loves us so much he won't let us stay attached to any kind of sin, including minor ones, for all eternity.

WHAT IS PURGATORY LIKE?

We don't know exactly what the process of purification includes or how long it will take. Jesus told the good thief on the cross, "Today you will be with me in Paradise" (Luke 23:43), and Pope Benedict XVI said, "The transforming 'moment' of this encounter eludes earthly time-reckoning—it is the heart's time, it is the time of 'passage' to communion with God in the Body of Christ."[138]

WHERE IS PURGATORY IN THE BIBLE?

If you wonder where purgatory is in the Bible, then also wonder about this—where does the Bible say all Christians immediately go to heaven after death?

Some people say the Bible teaches that "to be absent from the body is to be present with the Lord." In other words, after we die we will be "present with Christ" in heaven. But that is a misquotation of the Bible. In 2 Corinthians 5:8 St. Paul actually says, "We would *rather* [emphasis added] be away from the body and at home with the Lord."

If I say, "I'd rather be away from the office and at home with my family," that does not mean that once I step foot outside my office I will automatically be at home. Paul even tells us that after death we won't automatically have blissful rest with Christ in heaven. He says we will instead "appear before the judgment seat of Christ, so that each one may receive good or evil, according to what he has done in the body" (2 Cor. 5:10).

"The existence of a purgatory I have never denied. I still hold that it exists, as I have written and admitted many times."
—*Martin Luther*[139]

The Old Testament describes how Judas the Maccabee prayed for the souls of his slain comrades and "made atonement for the dead, that they might be delivered from their sin" (2 Macc. 12:45). Since prayers cannot help the damned in hell and are not needed for the saved in heaven, these prayers must have been applied to souls being cleansed of their sins after death in purgatory.

It's true that Protestants reject the inspiration of deuterocanonical books like 2 Maccabees, but they can't deny these books show how ancient Jews prayed for the dead so that their sins could be forgiven. In fact, Jesus taught about sins that are so serious they would not be forgiven in this life or "in the age to come" (Matt. 12:32). But this implies that "in the age to come," or the afterlife, there are less serious sins that can be forgiven, which happens in purgatory.

Perhaps the most striking text about the purification we will undergo after death is 1 Corinthians 3:13–15. In this passage, Paul refers to the testing of our works that will take place after death:

> Each man's work will become manifest; for the Day will disclose it, because it will be revealed with fire, and the fire will test what sort of work each one has done. If the work which any man has built on the foundation survives, he will receive a reward. If any man's work is burned up, he will suffer loss, though he himself will be saved, but only as through fire.

These verses unambiguously describe God's judgment after death and how our works will be exposed with fire. The fire may not be literal, because Scripture uses fire in metaphorical ways to describe cleansing and purification (Matt. 3:11–12). The text does say that when a man's inferior works are tested, the man being examined will suffer loss even though he will be saved.

What could that loss be given that he will be saved? The most natural interpretation is that the loss represents the suffering he will endure after death, as the negative effects of his inferior and wicked works are purged from his soul. He will be saved, but as through a purifying fire, or what we call purgatory.

MAKING AMENDS

It is natural for humans to want to make up for the wrong they have done, but no amount of work on our part can make up for the wrong caused by our sins against an infinitely holy God. (Only Christ's sacrifice can do that.) We can, however, make up for the temporal or earthly consequences of our sins.

Here's a way to understand the difference.

If my five-year-old son recklessly breaks a neighbor's window, I will pay for the window because he cannot. If my son is sorry for what he did then I will forgive him, but I will also ask him to perform extra chores to make up for his bad behavior. This satisfies his conscience's desire to make amends and also helps him learn a valuable lesson.

We might think discipline is the opposite of love, but if you've ever been around a spoiled child you see that the lack of discipline can make a person angry, frustrated, selfish, and just plain miserable. Since God is our loving father, he also graciously corrects us, or as the Bible says, "The Lord disciplines him whom he loves, and chastises every son whom he receives" (Heb. 12:6).

How does God our Father love us? "He disciplines us for our good, that we may share his holiness" (Heb. 12:10).

For example, God forgave King David for committing the sins of adultery and murder, but he disciplined David by allowing him to suffer in this life (2 Sam. 12:7-14). Indeed, whenever we sin we cause pain and suffering to other people, and we develop an unhealthy attachment to sin. Fortunately, through his Church God has given us a way to make up for the consequences of our sins and become holy just as God is holy (1 Pet. 1:16). This gift is called an indulgence.

Indulgences are not special "tickets" that help Catholics get into heaven or stay out of hell. Indulgences do not forgive sins and the Church has never sold them.[140] Instead, through sincere and specifically prescribed acts of faith and charity (like saying certain prayers or even reading the Bible), the Church applies the merits of Christ and the saints to us, so that we can be purified from the effects of sin *before* death instead of afterward. These merits can also be applied to souls in purgatory by praying and obtaining indulgences for them, just as we would pray for any Christian who is striving for holiness.

In Colossians 1:24 Paul said he made up in his suffering "what is lacking in Christ's afflictions." Since Christ's sacrifice is perfect, what Paul means is what is lacking is *our* sacrifice. God wants all of our sacrifices in this life to be united to Christ so that, as a family, we can help one another be full of grace and free from the effects of sin. That's why St. Paul says if we are children of God then we are both heirs of God, "and fellow heirs with Christ, *provided we suffer with him* [emphasis added] in order that we may also be glorified with him" (Rom. 8:17).

DOES PURGATORY TAKE AWAY FROM CHRIST?

If Christ's sacrifice is perfect and infinitely atones for sin, then why is purgatory even necessary? It's necessary because Christ's perfect sacrifice must be *applied* to each individual in different ways.

Those who reject Christ's offer of salvation, for example, won't have the saving effects of Christ's sacrifice applied to them. Believers who are attached to sin in this life will have the effects of Christ's sacrifice applied to them after death in purgatory. Theologians like Pope Benedict XVI have even speculated that the cleansing fire of purgatory is none other than Christ. He writes:

> Some recent theologians are of the opinion that the fire which both burns and saves is Christ himself, the Judge and Savior. The encounter with him is the decisive act of judgment. Before his gaze all falsehood melts away. This encounter with him, as it burns us, transforms and frees us, allows us to become truly ourselves.[141]

Purgatory doesn't take away from Christ's work, but rather *it is Christ's work*. It is not something the Church created in order to force people to work their way into heaven. Purgatory is instead something God created so that the grace his Son obtained for us on the cross could make us "holy and blameless and irreproachable before him" (Col. 1:22), free from the pain and penalty of sin, and ready to enter into eternal glory with Christ our Lord.

WHY WE BELIEVE: PURGATORY

- ✧ Sin causes both a temporal and eternal harm to our souls that must be purged before we enter into heaven.
- ✧ Christ takes away the eternal punishment of sin, and it is through his grace that the temporal punishments of sin are removed in purgatory.
- ✧ Indulgences are a way we can remove the temporal punishment associated with sin for ourselves and for souls we pray for in purgatory.

19

Why We Pray to the Saints

IN THE WEEKS leading up to my reception into the Catholic Church, I prepared to not only to be baptized, but also to be confirmed. The sacrament of baptism uses water to communicate grace that takes away sin, while the sacrament of confirmation uses hands that spread oil across the forehead. This oil seals the person with the gifts of the Holy Spirit in order to help him live out the Catholic faith. Hebrews 6:2 alludes to this sacrament when it says how, after baptism, we receive "the laying on of hands."

In some churches confirmation candidates choose a new name for the ceremony, which is usually the name of a saint who prays for that person. A lot of people pick a saint they can identify with, so, since I used to be someone who mocked the Christian faith but now enjoyed defending it, I chose St. Paul. He was, of course, a Jewish leader who used to kill Christians, but after an encounter with the risen Jesus, he became one of the Faith's greatest defenders (Phil. 3:3–11).

After our preparation class, one of the volunteers said to me, "You chose Paul as your confirmation name? Those are pretty big shoes to fill." I wanted to say "I've got big feet!" but instead I admitted, "I know, that's why I need his prayers."

ONLY ONE MEDIATOR?

Many non-Catholics struggle with the concept of praying to saints because they think prayer and worship are the same thing. Since the Bible says we should only worship God, then shouldn't we only pray to God? But the word "worship" refers to giving someone "worth-ship," or the honor that person is due. We call judges "your honor," for example, as a way of paying them respect, but we don't treat them like gods.

"Prayer" comes from the Latin word *precarius* and refers to making a request for something. In Old English a person might have said to a friend, "I pray you will join us for dinner tomorrow night." They aren't worshipping their friend as a god, but simply making a request of them. Catholics do the same thing when they pray to saints; they don't honor them as gods but ask them for their prayers.

DEFINE IT

The Church uses three Greek terms to define the kind of "worth-ship" we should give to those who are in heaven.

- ***Latria:*** The adoration and praise reserved for God the Father, the Son, and the Holy Spirit.
- ***Hyperdulia:*** The honor given to Mary, the most blessed of God's creatures.
- ***Dulia:*** The honor given to saints and angels in heaven.

Why should we ask saints in heaven to pray for us when we can just pray to God instead? After all, 1 Timothy 2:5, says, "For there is one God, and there is one mediator between God and men, the man Christ Jesus." Catholics agree that it is great to pray directly to God, but if this argument were taken to its logical conclusion, then it would forbid asking *anyone* on earth to pray for us.

After all, why ask a friend on earth to pray for you when you can go directly to God? Of course, St. Paul encouraged Christians to pray for everyone (1 Tim. 2:1-4), so 1 Timothy 2:5 must mean that Christ is our one mediator of *redemption*. Jesus Christ is the only person who unites man and God to one another and removes the barrier of sin between them. But Christ's unique role as our redeemer does not prevent us from mediating or interceding for one another—either in this life or the next one.

All Christians are united to one another because we are all members of the one body of Christ. Romans 12:5 says, "We, though many, are one body in Christ, and individually members one of another." If the saints in heaven are Christians, then they must belong to the same body of Christ to which all other Christians belong. This means Christians in heaven are united in the bond of love with Christians on earth, and so there is nothing wrong with asking them to pray for us.[142]

ARE THE SAINTS ALIVE OR DEAD?

It doesn't make sense to say Christians who are in heaven are some kind of "amputated" part of Christ's body that cannot pray for any of the other parts. Jesus calls himself the vine and says we are the branches (John 15:5). If Jesus holds the "keys of Death" (Rev. 1:18), then how could death ever completely separate the branches from one another as long as they are all spiritually connected to the same vine?[143]

Jesus said that God "is not the God of the dead, but of the living," and reminded his Jewish audience that the Father said, "I am [not "I was"] the God of Abraham, and the God of Isaac, and the God of Jacob" (Mark 12:26-27). In the time of

Christ (as well as the time of Moses), the Father was still the God of Jewish heroes like Abraham, who had died centuries earlier. To write off saints like them as being "dead" ignores the fact that, by virtue of their heavenly union with Christ, they are more alive than they were on earth.

In fact, Hebrews 12:1 provides an explicit reference to the saints in heaven having knowledge of what happens on earth. Hebrews 11 praises Old Testament figures like Abraham, Moses, and David, but then, in the first verse of chapter 12 (which in the original work was not separated into chapters), the author says, "Therefore, since we are surrounded by so great a cloud of witnesses, let us also lay aside every weight, and sin which clings so closely, and let us run with perseverance the race that is set before us."

The Protestant Bible scholar William Barclay says of this passage: "Christians are like runners in some crowded stadium. As they press on, the crowd looks down; and the crowd looking down are those who have already won the crown."[144] The great figures of the Old Testament, which the Church will always honor as saints (CCC 61), are like members of a cosmic stadium cheering us to finish the race and "keep the faith" (2 Tim. 4:7) lest we be disqualified by our sins (1 Cor. 9:27).

HOW DO THE SAINTS HEAR OUR PRAYERS?

It might be difficult to understand how saints in heaven could hear our prayers by themselves, but for God nothing is impossible (Matt. 19:26). At Pentecost, God gave the apostles the ability to speak and understand different languages, so there's no reason to think he wouldn't give the saints this same ability (Acts 2:4-6). Moreover, if God will give us glorified bodies at the end of time, then why wouldn't he also give us glorified minds that can know much more than normal human minds?

1 Peter 5:8 also says, "Your adversary the devil prowls around like a roaring lion, seeking some one to devour." Remember that Peter's warning is given to all Christians in all times and all places. This means the devil, who is just a creature, has the ability to ensnare billions of Christians at the same time with unique temptations he has crafted for each of them.[145] If God's enemy can have knowledge of what billions of humans do in order to tempt them, then why wouldn't God's friends, the saints, have a similar kind of knowledge and use that knowledge to pray for us?

HEAVENLY HELP WANTED

If the saints in heaven are aware of what affects believers on earth, then this naturally leads to the question of whether we should ask them to pray for us. Some people say that praying to saints is not in the Bible so Christians should not do that. But the Bible doesn't record anyone praying the "sinner's prayer" ("Lord Jesus, I am a sinner. Please save me."), but that doesn't make it wrong to say that prayer.

The Bible teaches that the prayers of holy people are more effective than the prayers of less holy people. For example, after Job's friends sinned, God instructed them to have Job pray for them. That's because Job was a very good man and God would hear his prayers (Job 42:8-9). James 5:16 says, "The prayer of a righteous man has great power in its effects"—and who could be more righteous than the saints in heaven, who have been cleansed of all sin? Hebrews 12:23 refers to these people as "the spirits of just men made perfect," and Revelation 5:8 describes them offering our prayers to God.

Finally, just as Protestants don't worship the wooden crosses they pray in front of but use them as reminders of Christ's death and resurrection, Catholics don't worship statues of saints they bow or kneel in front of. They instead use these figures as an aid to prayer, and their posture is done out of respect to the figure being represented; it is not an act of divine worship. Bowing to someone who isn't God isn't always wrong because, for example, Jesus promised the Church that, at the end of time, he would take its enemies and "make them come and bow down before your feet, and learn that I have loved you" (Rev. 3:9).

In the third century, St. Clement of Alexandria said that when a Christian prays, "though he pray alone, he has the choir of the saints standing with him."[146] In fact, prayers found in Christian catacombs of the fourth century describe how people asked their deceased loved ones to pray for them. One inscription near St. Sabina's in Rome says, "Atticus, sleep in peace, carefree in your security, and pray earnestly for our sinful desires."[147]

Catholics simply continue the ancient Christian tradition of paying respect to and seeking intercession from the holy men and women who reign with God in heaven.

ASKING A SAINT FOR A MIRACLE

During the Korean War, Fr. Emil Kapaun served as a chaplain and would often celebrate Mass using the hood of his jeep as an altar. He also ministered to dying soldiers under enemy fire. When his unit was captured and put in a prison camp, Fr. Kapaun dug latrines, gave away his food, and performed many other acts of heroism to help the soldiers under his care. In 1951, Fr. Kapaun died in the Sombakol POW camp, but over fifty years later people are saying he has not stopped helping young men in need.

Chase Kear, a member of a Kansas Community College track team, suffered what seemed to be a fatal head injury during a pole vault. Since Fr. Kapaun had always helped young men in impossible situations, Chase's aunt asked people in her church to pray for his intercession (Fr. Kapaun also grew up in a nearby Kansas town). Seven weeks later, Chase walked out of the hospital and told his story to reporters, despite the fact that a large a part of his brain had been removed.[148]

Chase and his family credit the prayers of Fr. Kapaun for his recovery, and the Vatican is currently investigating the incident as evidence for a possible declaration of Fr. Kapaun's sainthood.

WHY WE BELIEVE: THE SAINTS

✧ The Bible teaches there is one body of Christ and the saints in heaven belong to it.

✧ Each member of Christ's body should pray for the other members.

✧ The saints in heaven can hear our prayers and their prayers are powerful because they are holy people.

20

Why We Honor Mary

A FEW MONTHS before I was received into the Catholic Church, my family experienced a crisis. I was in high school when my mother told me she had been diagnosed with a large tumor in her abdomen. She didn't know how much longer she had to live, and my dad wasn't in the best position to take care of me and my siblings.

I felt like the weight of the world was on my shoulders, so I told my mom, "I need to just go to Church to process all of this." She had left the Church a long time before, but understood it was important to me, so she nodded in approval. I gave her a hug, told her I loved her, and started walking to the church.

As I knelt in that dark, empty church, my hands were clasped tight and my eyes watched the candles by the altar flicker. I just kept asking God for everything to be okay. Then I saw a statue of Mary. I took a deep breath and prayed:

> Hail Mary Full of grace the Lord is with you, blessed are you among woman and blessed is the fruit of your womb Jesus. Holy Mary, Mother of God, pray for us sinners, now and at the hour of our death.

Devotion to Mary was the last hurdle I faced coming into the Catholic Church. At first, I feared that Catholics went overboard when it came to Mary and turned her into a rival goddess who took away glory from Christ. But the more I read Scripture the more I saw that Mary didn't take people away from Christ, she led people to him.

THE MOTHER OF GOD

The most important title the Church gives to Mary is also the one that explains why Mary matters so much to Catholics—*theotokos.* This Greek word means "God-bearer," but it is usually translated into English as "the Mother of God." Mary is praised above all of God's other creatures because she has the most intimate relationship with God. She gave birth to God, nursed God, taught him about life, followed him throughout his ministry, and was at the foot of the cross when Jesus, the God-man, died.

If Jesus is God and Mary is his mother, it logically follows that Mary is the mother of God.

At this point some people might say, "Mary didn't give birth to God, she gave birth to Jesus." Yes, but is Jesus God? Calling Mary the Mother of God doesn't mean that she created the Trinity or that Mary existed before God existed. Being a mother means conceiving and giving birth to a person. God is a Trinity of three divine persons: Father, Son, and Holy Spirit. One of those persons, the Son, became man and had a mother (Gal. 4:4). It logically follows that this woman, or Mary, is the Mother of God.[149]

Mothers don't give birth to "natures" or "humanity," they give birth to persons. The person Mary gave birth to was the divine second person of the Trinity, God the Son, whom she and Joseph named Jesus. Even Protestants understand that Mary should be praised in this way. Timothy George says, "Evangelicals can and should join the church catholic in celebrating the Virgin Mary as the mother of God, the God-bearer."[150] Martin Luther eloquently said, "Men have crowded all her glory into a single word, calling her the Mother of God."[151]

EVER-VIRGIN

When Catholics call Mary the "blessed virgin," they mean that not only did Mary never have sexual relations before she gave birth to Jesus, she never had sexual relations at all. She remained "ever-virgin" throughout her life. But doesn't Matthew 1:25 say Mary did not have relations with her husband "until" she gave birth to Jesus?

Yes, but the word "until" in that verse does not always imply a reversal of conditions. 2 Samuel 6:23 says, "Saul's daughter Michal bore no children from that day on until the day she died" (ISV), but that doesn't mean Michal had children *after* she died. Likewise, 1 Corinthians 15:25 says Christ "must reign until he has put all his enemies under his feet," even though Christ will still reign even after he has defeated all his enemies.

Matthew 1:25 simply says that Jesus was born of a virgin. Concerning this verse, the Protestant Reformer John Calvin wrote, "No just and well-grounded inference can be drawn from these words of the Evangelist . . . as to what took place after the birth of Christ."[152]

What about the "brethren of the Lord"? Matthew 13:55-56 describes the people of Nazareth saying of Jesus, "Are not his brethren James and Joseph and Simon and Judas? Are not his sisters with us?" But consider that Mary calls Joseph Jesus' father (Luke 2:48), even though Joseph was not Jesus' biological father. This means that Jesus' brothers and sisters may not have been his *biological* brothers and sisters, or had Mary as their mother.

The Greek word translated "brethren" in this passage is also used in the Bible to refer to cousins and nephews.[153] Matthew actually describes James and Joseph as the children of another woman named Mary (Matt. 27:56), and Mark refers to Jesus as "*the* son of Mary," rather than "*a* son of Mary." In fact, none of Jesus' brethren are ever called sons or daughters of Mary, and it was unlikely that Mary would have given birth to seven children who all survived past infancy in a harsh first-century world.

Therefore, we can conclude that these brethren were Jesus' extended relatives, perhaps his cousins. Joseph may even have been a widower who had these children from a previous marriage. This would explain why people from Jesus' hometown referred to Jesus as the "son of Mary," rather than by the more traditional "son of Joseph." This would indicate that Jesus was not a child from Joseph's previous marriage. Either way, the "brethren of the Lord" were not sons or daughters of the Virgin Mary.

Keep in mind that Mary's decision to refrain from sexual intimacy was not because sex is bad. It was because the act of the Holy Spirit "overshadowing" her (Luke 1:35) and her body becoming God's intimate dwelling place is so good! In the Old Testament, when a woman gave birth to a child she belonged to the father of that child. Since Mary gave birth to God's son she belonged to God and gave her whole life to him.[154]

Joseph was still Mary's lawful husband and he protected her in a culture that was often unfair toward women. However, he also understood that many of the normal conventions we associate with marriage would be different because his family was "the Holy Family," commissioned by God with raising the most important person who ever lived.

IMMACULATE CONCEPTION AND BODILY ASSUMPTION

The *Immaculate Conception* does not refer to Jesus' miraculous virginal conception in Mary's womb. Instead, the term means that Mary herself was conceived without the stain of original sin.

The normal means to be freed from original sin is through baptism, but God is free to give his grace to whomever he chooses. He knew from all eternity that Mary would say yes to being the mother of his Son, so when she was conceived, God gave Mary an abundant gift of grace. In Luke 1:28, the angel Gabriel says to Mary "Hail, full of grace, the Lord is with you!" The Greek word that is translated "full of grace" refers to having grace as an enduring, complete quality of a person.[155]

But doesn't the Bible say all people have sinned (Rom 3:10)? If that's true, then how could Mary have been immaculately conceived?

First, that passage refers to the truth that both Jews and non-Jews are sinners and need Christ. In Romans 9:11, Paul says that before Isaac and Esau were born they had done neither good nor bad. Millions of human beings die in infancy, long before they reach the age of moral accountability, and thus have never committed a personal sin.

But aren't all humans born with *original* sin? No, because Jesus was human and he was born without original sin. If we say that Jesus is the exception because he is God, or the new Adam whose obedience undid the crime of the first Adam, then we have room for another exception: Mary, the Mother of God and the "new Eve," whose obedience to God undid the curse brought about by the old Eve. In the second century, St. Irenaeus said, "The knot of Eve's disobedience was loosed by the obedience of Mary. What the virgin Eve had bound in unbelief, the Virgin Mary loosed through faith"[156]

Finally, God demonstrated his surpassing love for his mother by taking her body and soul into heaven at the end of her earthly life. In the Old Testament, God assumed, or took, the prophet Elijah's body and soul into heaven before he died (2 Kings 2:11). The Church teaches that Mary was also assumed into heaven, and Revelation 12:1 describes a woman in heaven clothed with the sun who gives birth to the Messiah. She appears right after a vision of the Ark of the Covenant, which carried God's word written on stone tablets. It would be fitting if this woman were Mary, for she is the Ark of the New Covenant, who carried within her body the word of God made flesh, Jesus Christ.

"ALL GENERATIONS WILL CALL ME BLESSED"

As I knelt in that darkened church and prayed the Hail Mary over and over again, I more clearly saw that Catholics weren't turning Mary into a God. The reason Mary is "full of grace," "blessed," "holy," and the "Mother of God" is because her son is Jesus Christ. (It's amazing that, for the rest of time, God the Son will not only have a human face and body, but will bear a physical resemblance to a human woman who lived around 2,000 years ago.) The only thing Catholics were "guilty of" was recognizing the awesome role Mary played in the history of humanity. In Luke 1:48–49, Mary herself says "all generations will call me blessed; for he who is mighty has done great things for me, and holy is his name."

Speaking of awesome mothers, a few weeks after my mom told me about her diagnosis she was released from the hospital. I was nervous until she gave me the news: the tumor was benign. It ended up being the size of a basketball, but it was benign. I prayed to God, "Thank you for letting me have my mom for a little longer," and to his mother I prayed, "Please lead me and my whole family closer to your son, Jesus Christ."

WHY WE BELIEVE: MARY

- Of all of God's creatures, Mary has the closest relationship with God because she gave birth to him.

- As the Mother of God, Mary remained a virgin her whole life, was conceived without original sin, and was assumed into heaven.

- Catholics honor Mary because she always leads us to her son, Jesus Christ.

PART 5

MORALITY & DESTINY

21

Why We Protect Life

In ancient Rome, fathers had almost unlimited rights over their families. These *paterfamilias*, as they were called, could even take their own infants and abandon them in the wilderness if they didn't want them. Sometimes a passing stranger would find these children and raise them as slaves, but more often the children would be ripped apart by animals or slowly die of starvation.

Amidst this horror, the members of a new religion called Christianity took a stand. Their catechisms forbade killing children before and after birth, and some believers even rescued abandoned infants and raised them as their own children.[157] Fathers in the Roman Empire had the right to choose what happened to their families, but Christians said no one has the right to "choose" to directly kill another innocent human being.

Today the killing of unwanted children still takes place, but it doesn't happen in the wilderness. Instead, it takes place in hospitals and clinics, where it's called the "right to choose." But just as it did 2,000 years ago, the Catholic Church opposes the killing of unborn human beings, and it does so with nonreligious arguments any reasonable person can appreciate.

IMPOSING MORALITY?

Some people say, "Don't like abortion, don't have one!" or, "Don't impose your morality on me!" But civilized people impose morality on one another all the time. We impose the view that stealing is wrong on shoplifters who think "it's not a big deal." We impose the view that child abuse is wrong on parents who think hitting their kids "is not anybody else's business." Furthermore, the Church does not *impose* morality. Instead, it gently *proposes* a way to live that treats all human beings with respect and kindness.

> "The State may not impose religion, yet it must guarantee religious freedom and harmony between the followers of different religions."[158] *—Pope Benedict XVI*

Once when I was giving a presentation at a secular university, a woman in the audience asked me if I would deny abortion to a pregnant woman who had three children she could barely feed. I agreed with her that poverty is incredibly difficult, but then I asked, "Would it be wrong for this woman to kill one of her born children, like say a two-year-old, in order to free up resources for her unborn baby?" She said, "Of course that would be wrong," to which I simply asked, "Why?"

"Because you can't kill *real* human beings," she replied.

That, rather than poverty, was the real issue. If the unborn are not *real* human beings, then abortion is just a routine surgery and personally opposing it would be as odd as personally opposing heart surgery. But if the unborn are human beings like you or me, then personal opposition to abortion is not enough. If we care about justice and equality, then we must change people's minds so that the lives of unborn children can be protected under the law.

HOPE FOR THE POST-ABORTIVE

The Church teaches that God's mercy and grace are never far from the man or woman who is sorry for being involved in an abortion procedure. In his encyclical *The Gospel of Life*, Pope St. John Paul II wrote this message for post-abortive women:

> Do not give in to discouragement and do not lose hope. Try rather to understand what happened and face it honestly. If you have not already done so, give yourselves over with humility and trust to repentance. The Father of mercies is ready to give you his forgiveness and his peace in the sacrament of reconciliation. To the same Father and his mercy you can with sure hope entrust your child. With the friendly and expert help and advice of other people, and as a result of your own painful experience, you can be among the most eloquent defenders of everyone's right to life.[159]

WHAT MAKES US HUMAN?

If the fetus or unborn child is growing, then he or she must be alive. If a fetus has human parents and human DNA, then he or she must be human. The human fetus is also not a body part like skin cells or sperm or an egg. It is a whole human being who just needs time, nutrients, and the right environment in order to develop into a fully grown human being (the same things you and I need to develop into fully grown human beings).

The standard medical text *Human Embryology & Teratology* states: "Fertilization [also called conception] is a critical landmark because, under ordinary circumstances, a new, genetically distinct human organism is formed."[160]

DEFINING LIFE

- **Embryo**: Greek word that means "developing one"; a human being from conception until the eighth week of life.
- **Fetus**: Latin word that means "young one"; a human being from the eighth week of life until birth.

Some people say that even if a fetus is a member of the human species, it is not a "person," or it is not "fully human." But what is a "person"? What makes us "fully human"“

If being able to think or feel makes someone a person, then newborns and certain disabled born humans would fail that test. Born babies can't think or feel more than nonhuman animals like cows or rats, but we treat those infants better than these animals just because they are biologically human. Since science proves that unborn children also belong to the human species, this means we should value unborn children in the same way we value newborns, and protect them from being killed through abortion.

Other people say that an unborn child isn't viable until birth, so it's not a person because it needs the mother's body in order to live. But what gives us the right to take a human being who can survive in one environment and place him in an environment where he can't survive? Imagine if a group of Martians teleported us to their planet, whereupon we suffocated due to the lack of oxygen. Would their actions be justified because earthlings aren't "viable" on Mars? Of course not! Just the same, unborn humans have the right to live in the environment that is designed to sustain their lives: their mother's womb.

At this point, some people say, "Fine, it is a baby. But I have the right to do what I want with my body."[161] But if that were true then doctors could not deny pregnant women drugs like thalidomide, which, while effective at reducing nausea in pregnancy, can also cause babies to be born without arms or legs. Even more absurd, there would be nothing wrong with taking a healthy, prematurely born infant out of a hospital incubator, reinserting him into his mother's womb, and then killing him, since a woman can do "anything" with her own body.

It's true that we have the right to control our bodies, but that doesn't give us the right to use our bodies to hurt other innocent human beings. This is especially true with the tiny, unborn human beings a man and woman helped to create. If we expect fathers to be responsible and pay child support for the children they create, then shouldn't we expect mothers to be equally responsible for those same children? Shouldn't they provide "child support" through bodies that are naturally designed to care for those children?

WHAT ABOUT IN THE CASE OF RAPE?

It is never a woman's fault if she has been raped and she should never be punished for what happened. Unfortunately, in our culture we sometimes blame women for crimes committed against them, and in other cultures women are executed for becoming pregnant through rape. That's barbaric and wrong; no innocent person should suffer for another person's crimes.

But what about the child conceived in rape? He is just as innocent as his mother and yet we say it is okay for him to suffer for another person's crimes. Instead, why don't we provide nonjudgmental, nonviolent care for the victims of rape and only punish those who are responsible for committing this act of violence?

MANUFACTURED BABIES?

Although the Church supports technology that helps parents naturally conceive children, it opposes in vitro fertilization, or IVF. This process involves mixing sperm and egg in a laboratory and then implanting the newly created human embryo into a woman's body. Sometimes this woman is the child's mother, but in many cases it is a stranger who acts as a "surrogate" womb for the baby.

The Church opposes IVF because children have a right to be conceived and grow in the wombs of their mothers. They should not be manufactured in a laboratory by technicians who treat them like a product. In addition, more than one embryo is usually created, which means the healthiest child gets to live while his brothers and sisters are destroyed.

Some people find it hard to understand the wrongness of killing embryos, because they imagine human beings are constructed in the womb the way a car is constructed in a factory. If we wouldn't say a car exists when the first nut and bolt are screwed together, then how can we say a human exists when the first cells come together? But this analogy is inaccurate, because humans aren't constructed objects; they're developing persons. Here's an example from law professor Richard Stith that illustrates the difference.[162]

In the twentieth century, Polaroid cameras printed their pictures on paper that was stored inside the camera. When the paper emerged from the camera after the photo was taken, the image looked like a brown smudge. After several minutes the image began to appear on the paper, until it was fully developed.

> **Everything that was a picture of the Loch Ness Monster was there in that photo, just as everything that is a new human being is present in tiny human embryos.**

Now, imagine you are on a boat on a famous lake in Scotland and you took a Polaroid picture of the Loch Ness Monster. You show the Polaroid to your friend, who then throws it overboard and says, "Too bad it was just a brown smudge and not the Loch Ness Monster."

How would you respond to your friend? You would be furious and shout, "No! That was a picture of the Loch Ness Monster; you just didn't give it enough time to develop for you to recognize it and now it's gone forever!"[163]

Likewise, an aborted embryo or fetus was a living human being who had simply not developed into the more recognizable "infant stage" of life. Destroying a human embryo or fetus doesn't end the life of a potential person; it ends the life of a person with great potential.

These little persons, who are in a stage of life we all went through, possess the same dignity that exists in every human being from conception to natural death. This dignity deserves to be recognized and respected under the law, which is why the Church fights for the right to life of all human beings, especially the weakest and most vulnerable ones.

THE ABORTIONIST WHO CHANGED HIS MIND

Dr. Bernard Nathanson was a doctor who oversaw 60,000 abortions: he even performed an abortion on his own son.[164] In 1969, he cofounded NARAL, an organization dedicated to overturning laws that banned abortion. However, in the 1980s Dr. Nathanson saw the overwhelming evidence from ultrasounds and fetal photography that showed how abortion destroys the lives of small human beings.

He later joined the pro-life movement and admitted that he and other abortion advocates lied about the number of women who died from illegal abortions in order to get the laws changed. He wrote, "It was always '5,000 to 10,000 deaths a year.' I confess that I knew the figures were totally false, and I suppose the others did too if they stopped to think of it. But in the 'morality' of our revolution it was a *useful* figure."[165]

Nathanson grew up Jewish but converted to Catholicism in 1996. He said, "I'm confident about the future, whatever it may hold, because I've turned my life over to Christ. I don't have control anymore, and I don't want control. I made a mess of it; nobody could do worse than I did. I'm just in God's hands."[166] The prayer card handed out at his baptism contained one Scripture verse: "God, who is rich in mercy" (Eph. 2:4).

Dr. Nathanson passed away on February 21, 2011.

WHY WE BELIEVE: PROTECTING LIFE

- ✧ Catholics do not impose morality but propose moral principles that treat all human beings with dignity and respect.
- ✧ Human embryos and fetuses are biological human beings. There are no morally relevant differences between born and unborn humans.
- ✧ The unborn are not potential persons but persons with great potential who are unjustly killed when they are aborted.

22

Why We Cherish Our Sexuality

SEVERAL YEARS AGO, a television show called *The Pickup Artist* would train socially awkward men in the "art" of seducing women, and then have them compete against one another. Each week the guys would be sent out, followed by hidden cameramen, and whoever could pick up the most women was the winner of that week's challenge. A friend called me up and told me I had to watch the most recent episode.

"Why would I want to watch a trashy show like that?" I asked.

"Because your sister is on the show this week!"

I turned on the television and there it was, an awkward guy wearing a giant cowboy hat trying to pick up my sister. I screamed, "Don't do it, sis! Don't give this sleazeball your phone number!" But she did.

OBSESSED WITH SEX?

A lot of people think the Catholic Church is obsessed with sex or teaches that sex is dirty. But as shows like *The Pickup Artist* demonstrate, it is actually our culture that is obsessed with sex. Think of magazines at the grocery store that promise "874 Tips for Great Sex!" Or the fact that 70 percent of television shows contain sexual content.[167] The Church only seems obsessed with sex because it must interact with a culture that is always talking about it.

And contrary to what some people think, the Catholic Church does not teach that sex is bad or dirty. Pope St. John Paul II even taught that men have a moral obligation to help their wives experience orgasms so that the sex between them can be a truly intimate union.

THE POPE ON MUTUAL SEXUAL JOY

"What does a celibate old man in Rome know about sex, anyway?" Actually, a lot! After he spent several years counseling married couples as a parish priest, the future Pope St. John Paul II wrote a book called *Love and Responsibility*. In the chapter on "sexology," he writes, "[I]t is necessary to insist that intercourse must not serve merely as a means of allowing sexual excitement to reach its climax in one of the partners, i.e., the man alone, but that climax must be reached in harmony, not at the expense of one partner, but with both partners fully involved."[168]

When people ask me why the Church teaches that sex outside of marriage is wrong, I don't say it's because sex is bad or makes someone "impure." I say instead, "It's because lying is wrong and God wants us to practice sexual honesty."[169]

THE MEANING OF SEX

In the second century after Christ, the Roman philosopher and emperor Marcus Aurelius described sex in this way: "It is the rubbing together of pieces of gut, followed by the spasmodic secretion of a little bit of slime."[170] Fast-forward 1,800 years and the philosopher Peter Singer fares no better. In his textbook *Practical Ethics*, Singer says the morality of sex is no different than the morality of driving a car since, in both cases, all that matters is being "safe." He even says, "The moral issues raised by driving a car . . . are much more serious than those raised by safe sex."[171]

But almost everyone knows that sex is more important than driving and that it isn't a mere recreational activity like going to the movies.

If I were to tell you I had seen 500 movies in my relatively short adult life, you would probably think nothing of it. On the other hand, if someone else said he had been sexually intimate with 500 people, most of us would be shocked. But if sex is no more special than driving, then why does such behavior shock us? After all, we aren't shocked by Uber drivers who have driven thousands of people, so why be shocked by individuals who have slept with the same number of people?

Or consider that one of the worst things you can do in a romantic relationship is "cheat," or be sexually intimate with another person. Most people would feel betrayed if their partner even *asked* to have a "meaningless" fling with someone else. But why? The only explanation is that sex can never be *objectively* meaningless. Instead, it has a sacred, unchanging meaning that is expressed through the language of the body.

For example, a handshake says, "Nice to meet you." A hug says, "I'm here for you." But what bodily action says, "I give my whole self to you. I want to become one with you and be with you for the rest of my life"? It makes sense that an idea as powerful as the permanent, faithful, and total gift of self to another person could only be physically expressed through the most powerful way to unite two people—sexual intercourse.

WHAT'S WRONG WITH PORNOGRAPHY?

What the Church believes about pornography is best summarized in a quote attributed to Pope St. John Paul II: "Pornography is not wrong because it shows too much, it is wrong because it shows too little." Pornography reduces people to objects that are only meant to satisfy the desires of a consumer. It also trains the user's brain to be excited by sexual novelty and by power over other people's bodies. But this attitude is disastrous in marriage, where joy comes from being a *gift of self* to one, irreplaceable person.

If you or someone you know struggles with porn, know that God loves you and wants to free you from this sin, and that there are steps you can take to make that happen. Aside from seeking God in the sacrament of confession, I'd recommend searching the Internet for Catholic "brain retraining" programs. These courses use exercises that "rewire" your brain so it can find pleasure in authentic sexual joy rather than the false promises of the pornography industry.

ONE FLESH

The Bible says that when God created Adam and Eve they "were both naked, and were not ashamed" (Gen. 2:25). God doesn't want us to be ashamed of either the bodies he gave us or the pleasure that comes from uniting those bodies with our spouse. God could have designed us to reproduce without sexual intercourse, but he specifically wanted husband and wife to become "one flesh" (Gen. 2:24, Matt. 19:6).

What does that mean?

Think about when a person receives a heart transplant. Even though the heart has different DNA, it becomes a literal part of the person's body. The body and the heart "become one" because they each contribute to something greater than themselves (in this case, keeping the person alive).[172]

Likewise, when a man and woman have sex, their reproductive systems, incomplete on their own, become complete by contributing to something greater than themselves. The couple's bodies become one because through every act of sex they are ordered toward the creation of a new human life.

OUR BODIES AS TEMPLES OF THE HOLY SPIRIT

"Do you not know that he who joins himself to a prostitute becomes one body with her? For, as it is written, 'The two shall become one. . . .' Do you not know that your body is a temple of the Holy Spirit within you, which you have from God? You are not your own; you were bought with a price. So glorify God in your body" (1 Cor. 6:16, 19-20).

Not every act will result in a child, but each act does express through the body what the couple already expressed through their wedding vows: I give my whole self to you and only you until "death do us part." In fact, sex has traditionally been called *the marital act* because every act of sex communicates marital love to another person.

This explains why cheating causes so many people to end a relationship: through their body, the cheating partner didn't just "secrete some slime" with another person. Whether they intended to or not, they used their body to communicate the most sacred form of love and commitment to someone else.

Even if a couple consensually has sex outside of marriage, their bodies still speak a lie to each other. No matter how much an unmarried person may say, "I'll love you forever," he or she is always free to walk away from the relationship. As I told a group of couples I was recently mentoring, "You don't need a divorce to break off an engagement." That freedom disappears, however, after a person *publicly* makes this promise in front of the community, the Church, the state, and before God.

After marriage, a couple's sexual union expresses the true reality of their lifelong, faithful bond to each other. The couple may even be blessed with what is the most obvious sign that sex is ordered toward a permanent, one-flesh union: a child who will usually outlive this love and be a witness of it to the whole world.

HOW FAR IS TOO FAR?

Even if it doesn't involve intercourse, other behaviors like genital stimulation and even heavy petting are only appropriate in marriage because they excite the body enough to make it ready to have sex.

Engaging in these behaviors while abstaining from sex is like driving up an on-ramp and then slamming on the brakes just before you reach the freeway. Outside of marriage these behaviors become another form of sexual dishonesty, and the more they are committed, the harder it becomes to unnaturally "slam on the brakes" and not allow them to fulfill their purpose through intercourse.

So the question we should ask is not, "How far can I go?" but rather, "What can I do to protect my beloved?"

On the other hand, when an unmarried couple conceives a child they often have to face the grim reality that, whether they like it or not, they have been forever joined not only to their partner (even if it's just as "the ex I had a baby with"), but to a third person. Unfortunately for that other person, the child, recent studies have shown that unmarried couples who conceive a child are much more likely to either break up or divorce after getting married than married couples who have a child.[173]

FEAR AND PERFECT LOVE

In 1 John 4:18 we read, "There is no fear in love, but perfect love casts out fear." This is why I will never regret waiting to have sex until marriage. When my wife and I came together for the first time, there was no fear of disease, no fear we'd have an unplanned pregnancy, no fear that I would leave her if she didn't meet my sexual needs, and no fear of what other people would think of us. In its place was simply the joy of knowing that not only were we *allowed* to freely give ourselves to each other, but that is exactly what *God wanted* us to do now that we'd become husband and wife.

God's plan for sex never included shame, disease, lies, heartbreak, abandoned children, or abortion. Human beings brought those things into sex through the sin of sexual dishonesty. If you or your significant other has already had sex, then I hope you will find healing and peace through the sacrament of confession and make a renewed commitment to practicing sexual honesty.

No matter what your past experience has been, God loves you and wants you to be happy by saving sexual intimacy for marriage. That way, if you are called to married life, your sexual intimacy won't be haunted with shame, but will be an occasion when you can always honestly say to your beloved: "I give my whole self to you, and only you, as long as we both shall live."

WHAT ABOUT HOMOSEXUALITY?

Once I was going for a jog in Balboa Park in San Diego when I noticed that the city's annual gay pride parade was passing through. I decided to ask people what they thought of the Christian protesters who had come out, and ended up having a conversation with three self-identified gay men. One of them asked me, "So what does the Catholic Church say about me being gay?" I answered:

"The Church makes a distinction between someone's desires and someone's actions. We can't control our desires, and so they shouldn't be central to our identity. You can't say someone is sinning just because they have certain desires because, like I said, you can't control them. So I wouldn't say that I'm straight or that you're gay, but that we are men made in God's image with different desires for sexual intimacy."

They nodded, so I continued.

"Our desires don't define us, but we can be held accountable for how we act on those desires. A husband might desire other women he's not married to, but that doesn't mean he should act on that desire. The Church teaches that we shouldn't use sex for something it wasn't meant for, which means it's wrong for anyone to engage in same-sex behavior—even if they're straight."

They raised their eyebrows at the unexpectedness of what I said, so I went on.

"For example, if a straight guy has been in prison for a long time and he just wants sexual release, he might have sex with a man, even though he's not gay. But that would be wrong, because sex isn't just for satisfying our urges. For me, the big question I ask when I think about tough issues like same-sex attraction is: What is sex for?"

To my surprise, one of the young men said, "Procreation?"

My eyes lit up.

"Yes! You can love anyone without having sex with him or her, but for me it makes sense that sex isn't an expression of just any kind of love. Instead, it is an expression of the love that only exists between men and women, and that reaches its fullness in the creation of a new human life."

Rather than be offended, these young men pondered what I said and seemed to appreciate the reasonableness of it, as well as the fact that I didn't just quote the Bible and rest my case. Before we parted ways I gave them the website of a Catholic group named Courage (www.couragerc.org).

Courage doesn't try to change people's sexual orientation. Instead, the members of this group help people who are attracted to members of the same sex to understand God's plan for them as a whole person, which includes their sexuality. They even produced a documentary called *Desire of the Everlasting Hills* that is about three people with same-sex attractions who returned to the Catholic Church. You can watch it for free online at https://everlastinghills.org.

WHY WE BELIEVE: SEXUAL HONESTY

- The Catholic Church does not teach that sex is bad or dirty, but rather that it is a very good gift God gave us.

- Sex expresses through the body the language of marital commitment by making a couple "one flesh." Sex outside of this context, including oral sex and masturbation, involves a lie, because the body expresses marital love outside the bonds of marriage.

- God's plan for sex and marriage is not meant to shame us, but to free us from shame and give us peace and joy in our most intimate relationships.

23

Why We Defend Marriage

A FEW YEARS ago I was researching the issue of marriage and came across a clip from the television show *Sesame Street*. It's a conversation between a little boy named Jessie and the character Grover. It begins with Grover asking Jessie, "Do you know what marriage is?" It continues this way:

Jessie: A marriage is when two people get married?
Grover: Yeah. That's good. That's marriage. What do they do when they're married?
Jessie: Kiss.
Grover: They kiss, yes; what else when they are married?
Jessie: Hug.
Grover: That's good. That's good. Anything else?
Jessie: Nope.
Grover: That's it?
Jessie: Yeah.
Grover: Are they friends also?
Jessie: Yeah.
Grover: Oh that's a lot in the marriage, isn't it? Kissing hugging, friends, helping, all that stuff. Yeah. Well, I guess that's what marriage is all about.

But this is not what marriage is all about. Why didn't Grover talk about the promise to be "true to you," in "good times and in bad, in sickness and in health," until "death do us part?" Why is there no mention of raising children or being a family? What *Sesame Street* is describing isn't marriage; it's cohabitation.

In contrast, the Catholic Church defines marriage as "the matrimonial covenant by which a man and a woman establish between themselves a partnership of the whole of life and which is ordered by its nature to the good of the spouses and the procreation and education of offspring."[174]

I know that's not the most romantic definition, but at its core this definition means that marriage is not just a legal *contract*. Instead, a Catholic marriage is a *covenant*, or a sacred pledge of loyalty between persons. In marriage, man and woman don't just give their legal consent; they give their whole selves to each other both for their good and the good of any children they may have.

That's why, in the face of tremendous opposition from the world, and even from other Christian denominations, the Catholic Church upholds God's plan for marriage to be *permanent* and *open to life*.

"TILL DEATH DO US PART"

In 1969, Ronald Reagan, then governor of California, passed the first state law allowing for no-fault divorce. Instead of having to prove one partner committed a fault such as adultery or abuse, a marriage could be ended simply because the couple had "irreconcilable differences." But what have been the consequences of this redefinition of marriage?

After hitting a highpoint in the 1980s, the divorce rate has returned to the level it was at prior to no-fault divorce. But that's only because more people are choosing not to marry—11 percent more people, to be precise.[175] But that doesn't mean an increased number of people have stopped engaging in the marital act.

In 1963, only 7 percent of children were born out of wedlock. Today, that number is 40 percent, and in some socioeconomic communities it's as high as 71 percent.[176] On average, one out of four children in the U.S. lives apart from his or her biological father.[177] Research has found that children from divorced or unmarried households are more likely to live in poverty and more likely to be abused than children from stable marriages.

THE BEST GIFT FOR A CHILD

Child Trends, a nonpartisan research group that has studied the family for the past four decades, says that children in households with married parents have "in general, better health, greater access to health care, and fewer emotional or behavioral problems than children living in other types of families."[178] In contrast, a child whose parents cohabit but aren't married is four times more likely to be abused. A child whose mother has a live-in boyfriend is *eleven times* more likely to be abused.[179] The best gift you can give your child isn't the latest toy or game; it's married parents who are willing to resolve their problems in a healthy way.

Aside from the evidence social science provides for the goodness of lifelong marriage, the Bible reveals that God's plan for marriage always involved permanence. Jesus said that when a man and woman marry, "they are no longer two but one. What therefore God has joined together, let not man put asunder" (Mark 10:8-9). To make his point even clearer he said, "Whoever divorces his wife and marries another, commits adultery against her; and if she divorces her husband and marries another, she commits adultery" (Mark 10:11-12).[180]

The Catholic Church allows for legal separation and even civil divorce if there are circumstances like spousal abuse.[181] However, if the couple are both baptized Christians, then, following what Jesus taught, they are still validly married and so the Church prohibits either person from getting remarried. Even if the marriage fell apart because of infidelity or abuse, sin cannot undo what God has joined together. But grace can overcome sin.

It gives divorced spouses the strength to bear the crimes committed against them, and it gives spouses whose marriages are in trouble the humility to seek spiritual and professional help. Marriage is not easy, but as St. Paul said, "I can do all things in [Christ] who strengthens me" (Phil 4:13).

DIVORCE AND ANNULMENTS

At this point some people will say, "I've known lots of divorced people who've gotten remarried in the Church. All they had to get was an annulment!" But annulments are not a Catholic version of divorce.

Unlike divorce, which tries to dissolve a valid marriage, an annulment recognizes that there was never a valid marriage in the first place. It may *appear* that the couple was married on their wedding day, but a necessary element of marriage was missing. This may include:

1. Understanding of marriage: You can't validly say "I do" unless you know what you're saying "I do" to. If a person attaches conditions to marriage ("I'll stay married as long as we live near my family") or does not understand he

or she are agreeing to be in a permanent, monogamous union that is open to life, then the marriage may be invalid, or never happened in the first place, and thus declared "null" (hence the term "annulment").

2. Consenting to marriage: If a person is coerced or marrying to please others, then he isn't free, and the marriage may therefore be invalid. The young man who marries his pregnant girlfriend out of fear of her family (in a "shotgun wedding") would be one example of lack of freedom. But the presence of a psychological disorder or even being drunk on one's wedding day could render a marriage invalid, since the person was not truly free to say "I do."

3. Being able to marry: If a person is already validly married, below the age of consent, or is related to the intended by blood or adoption (among other circumstances), then he or she may not be capable of making the commitment that marriage requires, and would thus render any future marriage invalid if those circumstances—what the Church calls impediments—remain.

WHY DO I HAVE TO GET MARRIED IN THE CHURCH?

Just as a civil marriage isn't valid unless it happens in the presence of a representative of the state (like a judge or an approved minister) and according to the law of the state, a Catholic marriage isn't valid unless it happens in the presence of the Church and according to the law of the Church.

Weddings must normally take place in a Catholic church (unless the bishop has granted an exception), because marriage is one of the most sacred responsibilities a person will undertake in life and so it should begin in a sacred place. The

Church also wants to make sure that the couple truly understands the vows of permanence, monogamy, and openness to the life they are agreeing to, which is why the Church normally doesn't allow weddings to take place in churches of other denominations or in secular places where its views on marriage aren't shared.

A Catholic who is married outside the Church would be in an invalid marriage (and thus would be sinning by having sexual relations). This situation can be resolved, however, by having the existing marriage convalidated, or officially recognized by the Church.

"FIRST COMES LOVE, THEN COMES MARRIAGE, THEN . . ."

The Church doesn't demand that married couples have enough children to form their own basketball team. It also doesn't tell them, like the nation of China tells its citizens, that there are a maximum number of children they are allowed to have. The *Catechism* simply says that parents should exhibit "generosity appropriate to responsible parenthood" (CCC 2368), and that they should not use immoral means, like abortion or contraception, to plan their families.

In fact, many popular forms of contraception—such as IUDs and even some hormonal birth control pills—can kill an unborn child by preventing him from implanting in his mother's womb as an embryo. But even if a contraceptive didn't have the potential to cause abortions (like condoms, for instance), it is still wrong, because it's another form of sexual dishonesty.

We've already seen how sex has an intrinsic, marital meaning. When an unmarried couple has sex, they physically express a vow, like permanence, that doesn't exist yet and so they communicate a lie with their bodies. One of the vows the Church asks couples to make on their wedding day is to "accept children lovingly from God."The couple doesn't have to try to conceive a child every time they are intimate; they just promise not to directly sterilize their intimacy through the use of contraceptives.

WHAT DOES THE BIBLE SAY?

Even though condoms were known to exist in ancient Egypt, the Jewish people believed fertility was a gift from God so they did not promote the use of contraception. In fact, the Bible only records one act of contraception, when Onan "withdraws" from sex before climaxing. Genesis 38:10 says, "What he did was displeasing in the sight of the Lord, and he slew [killed] him."[182]

But why can't the couple keep their vow to be "open to life" by using contraceptives only *occasionally*?

The answer is: For the same reason a couple can't keep their vow of being "faithful" or monogamous by only having affairs "on occasion." As we've seen, in order for sex to be a one-flesh union it must be a *total gift of self* (nothing, not even fertility, can be held back), and it must be ordered toward something beyond the husband and wife's private feelings. It must be ordered toward the creation of a new human life.

But if that's true, then how are couples supposed to follow the Church's teaching that they responsibly plan their families? The answer: natural family planning, or NFP.

ORGANIC FAMILY PLANNING

It always amazes me that the same people who worry about buying organic food at the grocery store usually have no objection to using hormonal contraceptives, which the American Cancer Society has classified as a group-one carcinogen (or something known to cause cancer in humans).[183] That's why I love that NFP is an all-natural, latex-free, hormone-free way for my wife and I (along with millions of other couples) to space our children's births.

While men are usually fertile until they have one foot in the grave, women's fertility sharply declines later in life and is only present for a set number of days each month. NFP uses fertility tracking technology so if a couple wants another baby, they can choose to be intimate on a woman's identifiable fertile days. On the other hand, if they don't feel ready for another baby, they would simply choose to be intimate on an infertile day instead.

NFP requires both partners to work together to track fertility and decide when to be intimate. And to be honest, waiting for infertile days can be difficult. However, in my short time being married I've seen how the patience and communication NFP forces couples to practice helps to resolve conflict and improve marital health. Maybe this is why couples who use NFP have divorce rates between just 1 and 3 percent.[184]

But isn't NFP just a Catholic version of contraception? In both cases, the couple does something so that they don't have a baby. Although they appear to be the same, they are not. Here's an analogy that explains the difference, and why NFP is moral and contraception is not.

Imagine you are trying to select a wedding date and it's right around the time your wife's high-school-age cousins have a big football game. If you really want them to attend the wedding, you'll pick the week before their game. But let's say your budget is tight and you have no more room on your guest list. You might choose to schedule the wedding during their big game and send an invitation anyway as a sign that you still value the relationship. If they show up, it might be a bit stressful, but you'll be glad they came.

Now, let's imagine you don't want to wait a week and you *absolutely* don't want the cousins to come to the wedding. In order to make sure they don't arrive, you send them a "dis-invitation" that says, "Please don't come to our wedding, you're not wanted here!"

How does this relate to NFP?

Picking the date that works best for the cousins is like being intimate on a fertile day; you've created optimal conditions for children to arrive. Postponing the wedding by a week is like waiting to be intimate on an infertile day. The children probably can't arrive, but if they do that's still great!

Sending a dis-invitation, however, is like using contraception. Just as you'd be telling your cousins, "We want *this day,* so don't show up and ruin it!" using contraception sends the message to your future child (as well as God, who is responsible for every blessing of pregnancy), "We want sexual pleasure *at this specific time,* so don't show up and ruin it!" But children don't ruin sexual pleasure, they are its fulfillment, so we should never engage in an activity that sends the message that a child God may choose to bless us with is unwanted.

MARRIED SAINTS?

In 2015 Pope Francis canonized the first modern married couple, Louis and Zelie Martin. He said they "practiced Christian service in the family, creating day by day an environment of faith and love which nurtured the vocations of their daughters, among whom was Saint Thérèse of [Lisieux]."[185]

It's not uncommon for marriages to be strained after the death of a child, and the Martins endured the deaths of four infant children. Rather than give into despair, they lived as a model of married holiness for their five surviving children. Their days were divided into time for prayer, garden work, and relaxation, much of it in the countryside where Thérèse inherited her father's love of flowers and nature.

After his wife passed away, Louis struggled with loneliness as each of his five daughters joined the convent and became nuns. He still said, "It is a great, great honor for me that the Good Lord desires to take all of my children. If I had anything better, I would not hesitate to offer it to him."[186]

WHY WE BELIEVE: MARRIAGE

- ✧ Marriage is not a legal contract between two adults, but a sacred covenant between man and woman that, between baptized Christians, is an indissoluble union.
- ✧ A married couple always renews their marital vows in sexual intimacy, including the vow to "accept children lovingly from God."
- ✧ To responsibly space births, couples are encouraged to use methods like natural family planning, that do not harm either spouse or contradict the sacred meaning of the marital act.

24

Why We Believe There's a Hell

"WHAT YOU PEOPLE do is child abuse! You should be ashamed of yourselves!" a woman screamed at me while I was engaged in evangelism at a college campus.

I was genuinely confused so I asked her, "What exactly should I be ashamed of?" She fired back, "Hell! Telling little children they might go to hell traumatizes them!"

I'll admit this scares me! It's almost too difficult to imagine the possibility of being in agony not just for a while, but forever, living in despair and pain without end. And yet we can't reject hell just because we don't like it. Just as it's not child abuse to warn children about "stranger danger" or what will happen if they run into traffic, even if the truth is scary, it's not child abuse to warn children (or adults) about the dangers of hell—provided that hell is real.

WHO BELIEVES IN HEAVEN AND HELL?

Fifty-eight percent of Americans believe in hell and 72 percent believe in heaven. Even among nonreligious people, 36 percent believe in hell and 50 percent believe in heaven.[187]

WHAT THE HELL?

In the New Testament, the word "hell" usually refers to the final, eternal dwelling place for the damned.[188] According to the *Catechism*, "To die in mortal sin without repenting and accepting God's merciful love means remaining separated from him forever by our own free choice. This state of definitive self-exclusion from communion with God and the blessed is called 'hell'" (CCC 1033).

Scripture uses a variety of images to describe the awfulness of hell. Christ said it was a place of fire (Matt. 5:22), undying worms (Mark 9:48), gnashing of teeth (Matt. 13:42), and an outer darkness (Matt. 22:13). Matthew even compared it to Gehenna (Matt. 23:33), which was a place where children were offered as fire sacrifices to pagan gods.[189] Since Jesus walked out of his own tomb, he is a reliable source about the afterlife, and so we should believe what he taught about hell.

While Christ used earthly images to convey spiritual truths, we must remember that none of these images, including those of unending fire, are necessarily literal descriptions of hell. But even if hell is not a place of literal fire, it is still the worst thing we can imagine. Those who think hell is fun because all the "cool sinners" will be there should think again.

The sins that make life miserable, like selfishness, greed, hatred, and the vindictive desire to hurt others because we've been hurt, are just some of the evils that make hell so "hellish." In hell, sinners will eternally receive the one thing they cared the most about in life—themselves. Pope St. John Paul II said,

> The images of hell that Sacred Scripture presents to us must be correctly interpreted. They show the complete frustration and emptiness of life without God. Rather than a place, hell indicates the state of those who freely and

definitively separate themselves from God, the source of all life and joy.[190]

DOES HELL LAST FOREVER?

The most terrifying aspect of hell is its permanence. According to the *Catechism*, "The chief punishment of hell is eternal separation from God, in whom alone man can possess the life and happiness for which he was created and for which he longs" (CCC 1035). Jesus taught that hell is not temporary but lasts forever. He said that those who are damned "will go away into eternal punishment, but the righteous into eternal life" (Matt. 25:46).[191]

Some argue that if God were fair, then hell would be temporary and someone could eventually "work themselves" out of it. But no one can ever work himself out of hell any more than he could work himself into heaven. Salvation is a gift from God that we "work out" in this life (Phil. 2:12) by persevering in faith that works through love (Gal. 5:6) until the end of our lives (Matt. 10:22). The only time we can accept this gift, or this free offer of grace from God, is during our earthly lives. Upon our death, our choices in this life forever seal what our destinies will be in the next life (Heb. 9:27).

Moreover, if hell were temporary, it would be incredibly unjust. Since heaven includes eternal bliss and happiness with God, then no matter how long a person spends in hell it will seem like only a few seconds compared to the infinite happiness that awaits them in heaven. It would be like telling a child who purposefully breaks his sibling's arm that he has to go to "time out" for thirty seconds before he can go to an amusement park for the rest of the day.

Hell may also be eternal because the damned continue to sin and reject God after death. In this scenario, their punishment is everlasting because *they* make it that way and cannot do otherwise. If you've ever been around a self-centered person, you know he finds it excruciating to be in the presence of a person everyone else admires more. The damned in hell may even love themselves and their sins so much that the selfless love of God may be unbearable to them. They may even choose to remain in hell, thinking it is better than heaven.

WHAT ABOUT REINCARNATION?

After death the soul proceeds to heaven, hell, or purgatory; it does not return to earth to inhabit another body or become reincarnated. We can know this from the testimony of Scripture, Sacred Tradition, and even human reason.

First, humans do not behave as if they possessed souls that lived before the birth of their bodies. The third-century ecclesial writer Tertullian put it this way, "If souls depart at different ages of human life, how is it that they come back again at one uniform age? For all men are imbued with an *infant soul* at their birth. But how happens it that a man who dies in old age returns to life as an infant?"[192]

Second, if proponents of reincarnation are correct and souls are never created or destroyed but are only "reborn" into other bodies, then why has the human population been growing over time? This can only be explained by the creation of new human souls rather than the reincarnation of the same group of souls into different bodies.

Finally, if our memories from our previous lives are lost when we reincarnate, then, in the words of St. Irenaeus, "How do advocates of reincarnation know we've all been reincarnated?"[193] It makes more sense to believe, as Hebrews 9:27 teaches, that, "it is appointed for men to die once, and after that comes judgment."

IS HELL UNFAIR?

Many people ask, "How could a loving God send someone to hell?" But this question, as honest and important as it is, displays a mistaken view of the relationship between earthly choices and eternal destinies. The *Catechism* says, "God predestines no one to go to hell; for this, a willful turning away from God [a mortal sin] is necessary, and persistence in it until the end" (CCC 1037).

Hell is not something God created for the purpose of arbitrarily punishing people. Instead, *humans* created the necessity for hell through sinful choices that separated them from God. The Bible says that God is love (1 John 4:8) and God wants all men to be saved (1 Tim. 2:4), but love is free. God does not save people who don't want to be saved from their sins. According to the *Catechism*, "We cannot be united with God unless we freely choose to love him. But we cannot love God if we sin gravely against him, against our neighbor or against ourselves" (CCC 1033).

Another objection to hell is that it's unfair to inflict an infinite punishment for a finite crime. But the length of time it took to commit a crime does not indicate what the punishment for the crime should be. After all, a parking violation could happen over a period of hours while a murder could happen in a few seconds. It is the *nature* of the crime and the *intention* of the criminal that are relevant in deciding what the punishment should be.

THE REALITY OF THE DAMNED

"There can be people who have totally destroyed their desire for truth and readiness to love, people for whom everything has become a lie, people who have lived for hatred and have suppressed all love within themselves. This is a terrifying thought, but alarming profiles of this type can be seen in certain figures of our own history. In such people all would be beyond remedy and the destruction of good would be irrevocable: this is what we mean by the word *hell*."[194] —*Pope Benedict XVI*

But are the crimes in this life really so serious that they deserve infinite punishment in the next? Many people are willing to accept that while very awful people like genocidal dictators or sadistic serial killers deserve to go to hell, regular "good people" who commit "everyday" sins do not. But what makes someone a good person?

Does she give 20 percent of her income to charity? Does he ever gossip about people or break a promise? In his letter to the Galatians, St. Paul said that everyday sins like jealousy, anger, selfishness, sexual immorality, and drunkenness can prevent an otherwise good person from going to heaven (Gal. 5:19-20).

It's easy to define our own standard of a good person so that we always "clear the bar," but it's harder to meet Jesus' standard. He said, "You, therefore, must be perfect, as your heavenly Father is perfect" (Matt 5:48). No matter how hard we try, none of us is "good enough" to get to heaven on our own. That's why we need the free gift of God's grace so that we can be transformed not into "good people," but into "God's people," who share his divine life and are prepared in this life to be able to receive his unending love for all eternity.

A CHILD ALIVE AGAIN

In the Gospels, Jesus told a parable about a son who left home and squandered the money his father gave him. He became so poor he nearly starved to death, but he didn't think his father would let him come home. He hoped that maybe his father would let him work as a servant so he could at least have something to eat.

The son then decided to make the journey home, and Jesus says, "While he was yet at a distance, his father saw him and had compassion, and ran and embraced him and kissed him" (Luke 15:20). The Father then threw a party for the son because, as he says, "my son was dead, and is alive again; he was lost, and is found" (Luke 15:24).

This is called the parable (or story) of the prodigal son. Many people, including non-Christians, have heard it, but there's a detail that often gets missed: the father sees the son at a distance. This is probably because the father kept watch every day, waiting for his son's return. Imagine the joy he felt when he recognized the far-off figure was his son—alive and safe in his arms again!

Like the father of the prodigal son, God won't force us to love him or obey him. This is why hell is a real possibility for those who choose selfishness and sin over love and holiness. But like the father in the parable, God is always waiting for us to come home to him. That's why 2 Peter 3:9 says that God is patient with us, "not wishing that any should perish, but that all should reach repentance."

WHY WE BELIEVE: HELL

- ✧ Since God is love, he never forces anyone to love or obey him, but allows those people to live apart from him for all eternity, a state that is called hell.

- ✧ Since God is just, he punishes evil by allowing unrepentant sinners to choose their sin over his goodness and life.

- Since God is merciful, he gives everyone an opportunity to know him, reject sin, and choose eternal life through his son, Jesus Christ.

25

Why We Hope for Heaven

THE FAMOUS EVANGELIST Billy Graham once visited a small town to preach at the local church. Before he went to the church he needed to mail a letter back home, so he went looking for the post office. He pulled his car over to the side of the road and asked a boy walking his dog where it was and the boy politely answered.

Mr. Graham then invited the boy to attend the church where he'd be preaching. He said, "You can hear me telling everyone how to get to heaven." The boy simply replied, "I don't think I'll be there. You don't even know your way to the post office!"[195]

WHAT IS HEAVEN LIKE?

"How do I get to heaven?" is one of the most important questions a person can ask. But what do we mean by the word "heaven?"

In some cases, the Bible uses the word "heaven" to refer to the sky, or to the place of the sun, stars, and moon. This is seen in passages like Psalm 19:1, which says, "The heavens are telling the glory of God." Other times, "heaven" refers to the place where God dwells, as in the Lord's Prayer, where we address "Our Father who art in heaven" (Matt. 6:9). Finally, "heaven" is used to refer to the eternal dwelling place of those who love God. St. Paul says, "Our citizenship is in heaven. And we eagerly await a Savior from there, the Lord Jesus Christ" (Phil. 3:20, NIV).

Many people imagine this heaven to be a place in the clouds where saints and angels play harps for all eternity. But while the Bible does use earthly imagery like wedding feasts to describe heaven, the *Catechism* says, "This mystery of blessed communion with God and all who are in Christ is beyond all understanding and description" (CCC 1027). Paul, quoting the promises given to the prophet Isaiah, said, "No eye has seen, nor ear heard, nor the heart of man conceived, what God has prepared for those who love him" (1 Cor. 2:9).

Our inexact knowledge of heaven does not mean that we are ignorant of heaven in general. According to Pope St. John Paul II, "The 'heaven' or 'happiness' in which we will find ourselves is neither an abstraction nor a physical place in the clouds, but a living, personal relationship with the Holy Trinity."[196] In heaven we won't be angels; we will be reunited with our bodies and will experience both spiritual and physical joy in the presence of God. The *Catechism* teaches us, "Heaven is the ultimate end and fulfillment of the deepest human longings, the state of supreme, definitive happiness" (CCC 1024).

"THEN I SHALL UNDERSTAND FULLY"

St. Paul once compared our knowledge of God in this life to our knowledge of ourselves when we see our reflection in a dirty bronze mirror. At this time in history glass mirrors were just beginning to be invented and were not as popular as polished metal. He said, "For now we see in a mirror dimly, but then

face to face. Now I know in part; then I shall understand fully, even as I have been fully understood" (1 Cor. 13:12). Because of sin and our fallen human natures, we only perceive God indirectly; our relationship with him lacks the intimacy and wonder that it will have in heaven.

Heaven won't be an eternally long Church service; that would be as insufferable as hell. In fact, any earthly activity, be it a Church service, a rock concert, or a day at an amusement park, would be hellish if it were drawn out over an infinite period of time. Heaven won't consist of unending earthly joys, because these finite things can't satisfy our longing for perfect and unending happiness.

But God, who is infinite goodness itself, is the only reality that can provide us with the perfect love and understanding our hearts desire. In heaven, believers will adore God for all eternity and never reach an end or stagnant plateau of what they adore.

CAN ANYONE GET TO HEAVEN?

St. Paul says that even though non-Jews were not given written, divine revelation, God would judge them on the basis of another law. Paul says, "What the law requires is written on their hearts, while their conscience also bears witness and their conflicting thoughts accuse or perhaps excuse them on that day when, according to my gospel, God judges the secrets of men by Christ Jesus" (Rom. 2:15–16).

Does this contradict Jesus' teaching that he is "the way, and the truth, and the life; no one comes to the Father, but by me" (John 14:6)? No, because acknowledging that Christ is the only *objective* way we are saved (i.e., only Christ takes away the sins of the world) does not mean a person cannot be saved if he does not know this truth about Christ. For example, one could say antivenom is the only way to be saved from a snakebite, but a child receiving antivenom does not have to know this truth in order to be saved from the bite.

Similarly, a person could seek after "the way" or "the truth" and strive to act with perfect love, all without realizing that he was unknowingly seeking after Christ who is "the way, the truth, and the life." This also applies to non-Catholic Christians who do not understand the ordinary necessity of receiving sacraments like the Eucharist for salvation. The *Catechism* says that those "who believe in Christ and have been properly baptized are put in a certain, although imperfect, communion with the Catholic Church" (CCC 838).

But if people can be saved if they don't know Jesus or his Church, then why bother telling them about the Faith at all? Don't we risk their souls by giving them an opportunity to reject the gospel?

Consider this analogy. Imagine you are trying to help people cross over a river that has partially frozen over. The river is shrouded in fog and when people choose to walk across its icy surface they disappear into the mist. Did they make it across? It's *possible* they safely made it, but it's also possible, if not probable, that many of them did *not* make it across. Let's say, however, that you knew about a bridge that safely crosses over the river. Even if they might reject your offer, wouldn't you still tell people about this safer and more certain way to get across the river?

Preaching the gospel doesn't endanger souls because every person who never knew Jesus will not automatically go to heaven. Such people, like everyone else, are tempted by sin, and without God's grace it is even harder for these people to resist the devil's lies. The Church is, therefore, mindful of these people and so it, "fosters the missions with care and attention."[197] That's why Jesus commanded his followers to "make disciples of all nations, baptizing them in the name of the Father and of the Son and of the Holy Spirit" (Matt. 28:19).

WHY WE BELIEVE . . . EVERYTHING

My favorite description of heaven is from a homily I heard a deacon tell more than a decade ago. As a child, the deacon lived in Maine, and one winter he developed a severe case of strep throat and had to be hospitalized. His mother was usually at home caring for his siblings and his father had to travel for work. He loved reading the letters his dad sent from the road, but usually he spent a lot of time by himself listening to the radio or just staring out the window.

One day he woke up and it was quiet all around his hospital room. There didn't even seem to be anyone out in the hall. It was cold outside, but the rays of the sun warmed the floor by the window. He got out of bed, shuffled over to the window, and saw a car pull up beside a tree whose leaves were shedding.

As the orange and brown leaves gently fell to the ground, the little boy saw a man getting out. He was wearing a dark suit and a hat obscured his face. But when the man looked up, the little boy recognized it was his father, home early from his trip. His heart swelled with joy and he ran down the hallway and the stairs of the hospital. He leapt into his father's arms and shouted, "Daddy, you're home!"

The deacon then spoke about heaven and what people think it is. He hoped that at the end of his life he would be at home and would get to say goodbye to his wife, children, and grandchildren.

He imagined that after breathing his last breath, the next moment he would be opening his eyes and seeing the same ceiling over the same hospital bed he was confined to as a child (he even thought his throat might be sore from the cleansing he received in purgatory). All he would hear was the creaking of his bed as he placed his feet on the same tile floor warmed by the sun shining through the window.

With his hands pressed against the cool glass, he would see gently falling leaves and his father—but this time it would be his heavenly Father. Then he would run. His body would leap like he was ten years old again and in one embrace he'd feel the warmth of God's all-powerful love. Struggling to overcome his emotions, he holds tight, never wanting to let go again, and exclaims, "Daddy, I'm home!"

This is why we're Catholic. Not to follow arbitrary rules or rituals, but to go home. Everyone knows, deep down, that sin has wounded our relationship with God and with one another. We are Catholic because we want to give up the empty promises of sin and trust in God's promises to his family, which is united to him through the Church his Son gave us.

If you have been away from the Church, no matter how long, or even if you aren't Catholic, I'd like to invite you to experience God's love and discover his plan for you in the Catholic Church. I'd like to invite you to come home.

WHY WE BELIEVE: HEAVEN

- Heaven is the state of perfect happiness where we will adore and rest in God for all eternity.

- God will judge people on the revelation they've received and he extends his offer of salvation to everyone, even if they've never heard of Christ or his Church.

- Out of love for their fellow man, Christians are called to preach the gospel to the entire world so that anyone can have a personal relationship with Jesus Christ and find salvation through his Church.

How to Become Catholic

If you (or someone you know) are interested in becoming Catholic, seek out a nearby Catholic parish and inquire about its RCIA program. RCIA stands for "Rite of Christian Initiation for Adults" and has always been present, in some form, since the beginning of Church history, as a way of preparing adults and older children to enter the Church. It's also available to Catholics who have fallen from the practice of the Faith and want to come back, or who just want to learn more.

Prospective converts to the Catholic faith are called catechumens, which means "ones being instructed." A local priest or religious education director can determine what level of instruction a catechumen needs, but normally they will encourage the person to take part in a process that includes:

The Period of Inquiry: This time allows prospective converts to learn about the Catholic Church by attending Mass, spending time with the Lord in an adoration chapel, meeting with a priest or knowledgeable Catholic, or even by listening to Catholic radio or television. Above all else, the catechumen should pray for guidance through the RCIA process in order to develop a personal relationship with God through his son, Jesus Christ.

The Order of Catechumens: An inquirer who wishes to become Catholic enters the order of catechumens. In order to do this, he is required to select a sponsor, a practicing Catholic who will guide and support him through the process and will be present when he receives the sacraments of initiation.

Catechesis: The catechumen is formally taught the doctrines of the Faith and instructed in how to live the Christian life. This period culminates in the Rite of Election, where the Church formally recognizes a person's desire to become Catholic.

The Sacraments of Initiation: For most people, the RCIA process reaches its climax at the Easter Vigil, where non-Christian catechumens receive baptism, confirmation, and the Eucharist. Catechumens from other Christian denominations with valid baptisms receive confirmation and the Eucharist. It is a joyous occasion that celebrates how God has brought his children into full communion with Christ's "one, holy, Catholic, and apostolic Church."

How to Go to Confession

IF YOU ARE Catholic you can be at peace with God by confessing your sins in the sacrament of reconciliation, or what is often called confession. Before you receive the sacrament understand that God doesn't want to you to feel miserable for your sins: he wants to free you from them. But in order to do that, we must repent, or turn away from sin and turn toward Christ. The only way we can reject our sins is by identifying them and expressing our sorrow to God for having committed them.

In the sacrament of reconciliation you can confess any sin, but you must confess any mortal sins you've committed, or gravely evil actions you freely chose to take part in even though you knew they were wrong. These sins cut us off from a relationship with God, and so we must seek forgiveness for having committed them. One way to determine if you've committed a mortal sin is to conduct an "examination of conscience." These practical guides, which can be found online, ask a series of questions that help us see if we have committed a mortal sin. Here are some examples of sins that can be mortal, and thus need to be confessed:

1. Denying God exists or rejecting the Catholic faith

2. Taking God's name in vain or failing to go to Mass on Sunday and other important Holy Days

3. Disrespecting or failing to care for one's parents

4. Murder, abortion, or intense hatred of others

5. Adultery, sex outside of marriage, the use of contraception, the use of pornography, getting married outside of the Church, or engaging in homosexual behavior

6. Stealing that causes serious harm

7. Lies or even gossip that cause serious harm

After you've examined your conscience, you are ready to receive the sacrament of confession. Most Catholic churches offer this sacrament on a certain day of the week, which can be found on the church's website or by calling the parish office. In the church, there will usually be a room off to the side with a sign indicating that it is where confession is held. Don't worry if it's been a long time or if you've never been to confession. The priest will help you through any part of the sacrament you aren't familiar with, but here are the basic steps to remember:

1. **Introduction:** You can speak to a priest directly or from behind a curtain to remain anonymous. Begin by saying, "Bless me Father, for I have sinned. It has been [insert amount of time] since my last confession.

2. **Confession:** Keep it simple and just say what sins you committed and how many times you committed them. Don't worry about explaining unnecessary details or why you sinned, you just need to tell the priest your sins and say you're truly sorry. If you can't remember how

many times you committed a sin, give an estimate. If you desire further counseling, call the church office and an appointment can usually be made so you can discuss these issues with a priest at greater length.

3. **Contrition:** The priest will then ask you to say an Act of Contrition. Here is one many Catholics use: "My God, I am sorry for my sins with all my heart. In choosing to do wrong and failing to do good, I have sinned against You, whom I should love above all things. I firmly intend, with your help, to do penance, to sin no more, and to avoid whatever leads me to sin. Our Savior Jesus Christ suffered and died for us. In his name, my God, have mercy."

   Don't worry about memorizing this prayer as it is usually posted in the confessional for you to recite (though it's still a good prayer to memorize).

4. **Penance:** The priest will suggest something for you to do, such as a series of prayers, to make up for the consequences of your sins. Only Christ can make up for the eternal consequence of our sins, but through our prayers and works we can make up for the harm our sins cause in this life. Remember the penance you're given and complete it soon after your confession.

5. **Absolution:** The priest will then offer a prayer of absolution, through which God will forgive you your sins. He will usually say this: "God, the Father of Mercies, through the death and resurrection of his Son, has reconciled the world to himself and sent the Holy Spirit among us for the forgiveness of sins. Through the ministry of the Church, may God grant you pardon and

peace. And I absolve you from your sins in the name of the Father, and of the Son, and of the Holy Spirit. Amen." You respond by saying, "Amen."

6. **Conclusion:** The priest will probably say something like, "Go in peace," to which you can respond "Amen" or "Thanks be to God."

Common Catholic Prayers

SIGN OF THE CROSS

In the name of the Father, and of the Son, and of the Holy Spirit. Amen.

OUR FATHER

Our Father, who art in heaven, hallowed be thy name; thy kingdom come; thy will be done on earth as it is in heaven. Give us this day our daily bread; and forgive us our trespasses as we forgive those who trespass against us; and lead us not into temptation, but deliver us from evil. Amen.

HAIL MARY

Hail Mary, full of grace. The Lord is with thee. Blessed art thou among women, and blessed is the fruit of thy womb, Jesus. Holy Mary, Mother of God, pray for us sinners, now and at the hour of our death. Amen.

GLORY BE

Glory be to the Father, and to the Son, and to the Holy Spirit. As it was in the beginning, is now, and ever shall be, world without end. Amen

APOSTLES' CREED

I believe in God, the Father almighty, Creator of heaven and earth, and in Jesus Christ, his only Son, our Lord, who was conceived by the Holy Spirit, born of the Virgin Mary, suffered under Pontius Pilate, was crucified, died, and was buried; he descended into hell; on the third day he rose again from the dead; he ascended into heaven, and is seated at the right hand of God the Father almighty; from there he will come to judge the living and the dead. I believe in the Holy Spirit, the holy catholic Church, the communion of saints, the forgiveness of sins, the resurrection of the body, and life everlasting. Amen.

PRAYER BEFORE MEALS

Bless us O Lord, and these thy gifts, which we are about to receive, from thy bounty, through Christ, our Lord. Amen.

PRAYER TO OUR GUARDIAN ANGEL

Angel of God, my guardian dear, to whom God's love commits me here, ever this day be at my side to light and guard, to rule and guide. Amen.

MORNING OFFERING

O Jesus, through the Immaculate Heart of Mary, I offer you all my prayers, works, joys, and sufferings of this day, for all the intentions of your Sacred Heart, in union with the holy sacrifice of the Mass throughout the world, in reparation for my sins, for the intentions of all my relatives and friends and in particular for the intentions of the Holy Father.

EVENING PRAYER

O my God, at the end of this day I thank you most heartily for all the graces I have received from you. I am sorry that I have not made a better use of them. I am sorry for all the sins I have committed against you. Forgive me, O my God, and graciously protect me this night. Blessed Virgin Mary, my dear heavenly mother, take me under your protection. St. Joseph, my dear guardian angel, and all you saints of God, pray for me. Sweet Jesus, have pity on all poor sinners, and save them from hell. Have mercy on the suffering souls in purgatory.

Endnotes

Introduction: Why We Believe . . . Anything

[1] 1 Thessalonians 5:21.

Chapter 1: Why We Believe in Truth

[2] Only a few statements are *absolutely* true, or true in all times and all places. These include statements about logical contradictions like "there are no square circles" or "there are no married bachelors."

[3] "Penn Jillette gets the gift of a Bible." Available online at www.youtube.com/watch?v=6md638smQd8

Chapter 2: Why We Believe in Science

[4] St. Thomas Aquinas, *Summa Contra Gentiles*, 1:64.

[5] P. B. Medawar, *Advice to a Young Scientist* (New York: Basic Books, 1979), 31.

[6] Pope Benedict XVI, Meeting of the Holy Father Benedict XVI with the Clergy of the Dioceses of Belluno-Feltre and Treviso, July 24, 2007, www.vatican.va/holy_father/benedict_xvi/speeches/2007/july/documents/hf_ben-xvi_spe_20070724_clero-cadore_en.html.

[7] Sheila Rabin, "Nicolaus Copernicus," in Edward N. Zalta, ed., *The Stanford Encyclopedia of Philosophy,* Fall 2010 ed., plato.stanford.edu/archives/fall2010/entries/copernicus/.

[8] This is found in Niccolini's February 13 and April 16 letters in 1633 to the king of Tuscany.

[9] Pew Research Forum, "Scientists and Belief," November 5, 2009, www.pewforum.org/2009/11/05/scientists-and-belief/.

[10] J. L. Heilbron, *The Sun in the Church: Cathedrals as Solar Observatories* (Cambridge: Harvard University Press, 1999), 3.

[11] *Catechism of the Catholic Church* (CCC) 1814. The *Catechism* is a summary of what Catholics believe.

[12] See also CCC 142-165 for a more comprehensive description of faith from a Catholic perspective.

[13] I owe this example to philosopher Timothy McGrew.

Chapter 3: Why We Believe in a Creator

[14] This is called the Kalām cosmological argument. For more, see chapters nine and ten of my book *Answering Atheism* (2013).

[15] While the Big Bang is still the majority view, it is incomplete. Scientists have proposed new mechanisms such as "inflation" to account for irregularities in this standard model such as the flatness problem or the horizon problem. Scientists also need a quantum theory of gravity to account for the universe's structure at the Big Bang itself because relativity theory becomes incapable of describing the singularity prior to what is called the Planck time, or 10^{-43} seconds.

[16] Lisa Grossman, "Why Physicists Can't Avoid a Creation Event," *New Scientist Magazine*, January 11, 2012. In their original paper, Audrey Mithani and Alexander Vilenkin write, "Did the universe have a beginning? At this point, it seems that the answer to this question is probably yes." Mithani and Vilenkin, "Did The Universe Have a Beginning?," Cornell University Library, High Energy Physics—Theory, 2012, arxiv.org/abs/1204.4658.

[17] For more information, see John Farrell, *The Day Without a Yesterday: Einstein, Lemaître, and the Birth of Modern Cosmology* (New York: Thunder's Mouth Press, 2005), 115. Farrell cautiously notes, "There is some confusion as to the extent of Einstein's enthusiasm for Lemaître's primeval atom theory . . . Encouraging as Einstein was, it's unlikely that he regarded Lemaître's primeval atom theory as the last word on the subject—and unlikelier still that he would have employed the word 'creation' to describe it."

[18] Quoted in Michio Kaku, *Parallel Worlds: A Journey through Creation, Higher Dimensions, and the Future of the Cosmos* (New York: Anchor Books, 2005), 69-70.

[19] David Albert, "On the Origin of Everything: 'A Universe from Nothing by Lawrence Krauss,'" *New York Times Book Review*, March 23, 2012, www.nytimes.com/2012/03/25/books/review/a-universe-from-nothing-by-lawrence-m-krauss.html?_r=0.

[20] This is called the fine-tuning argument. For more, see chapters eleven and twelve of my book *Answering Atheism* (2013).

[21] Alexander Vilenkin, *Many Worlds in One* (New York: Hill and Wang, 2006), 10.

[22] Some people say our universe can be fine-tuned by chance if it is one universe within a larger collection of universes called the "multiverse." Within this collection there would be trillions of dead universes and

maybe just one universe like ours that has life. But aside from the lack of evidence for the multiverse, there are bigger problems with this explanation of fine-tuning. Paul Davies, an accomplished non-Christian physicist, explains: "Can the multiverse provide a complete and closed account of all physical existence? Not quite. The multiverse comes with a lot of baggage, such as an overarching space and time to host all those bangs, a universe-generating mechanism to trigger them, physical fields to populate the universes with material stuff, and a selection of forces to make things happen. Cosmologists embrace these features by envisaging sweeping 'meta-laws' that pervade the multiverse and spawn specific bylaws on a universe-by-universe basis. The meta-laws themselves remain unexplained—eternal, immutable, transcendent entities that just happen to exist and must simply be accepted as given. In that respect the meta-laws have a similar status to an unexplained transcendent god." Paul Davies, "Stephen Hawking's Big Bang Gaps," *Guardian,* September 3, 2010, www.guardian.co.uk/commentisfree/belief/2010/sep/04/stephen-hawking-big-bang-gap.

[23] Assume for simplicity that the odds of getting a royal flush are one in a million (it's closer to one in 650,000). The odds of getting fifty royal flushes in a row would be (1/10^6)^50, which leave us with 1/10^300. This comes nowhere near physicist Roger Penrose's number for the odds of our universe having low enough disorder to allow life to exist (1/10^10^123). Richard Dawkins, *The God Delusion* (New York: Houghton Mifflin Company, 2006), 147.

[24] Lisa Dyson, Matthew Kleban, and Leonard Susskind, "Disturbing Implications of a Cosmological Constant," Cornell University Library, High Energy Physics—Theory, 2002, arxiv.org/abs/hep-th/0208013.

Chapter 4: Why We Believe in God

[25] Aristotle, *The Metaphysics*, Book XII.

[26] CCC 239, 270.

Chapter 5: Why We Believe God Conquers Evil

[27] Nick Vujicic, *Life Without Limits* (New York: Doubleday, 2010), 34.

[28] J.L. Mackie, *The Miracle of Theism: Arguments For and Against the Existence of God* (Oxford: Oxford University Press: 1982), 115.

[29] Available online at http://www.africa.upenn.edu/Articles_Gen/Letter_Birmingham.html.

[30] Some people say that morality can't be grounded in God because

if God commanded us to do something evil, like torture a child, it wouldn't become moral just because God commanded it. Therefore, something over and above God must exist in order to ground morality and determine these acts are objectively evil. But because God is a perfect and infinite being who exists without limit or flaw, he will necessarily command only good acts that correspond with his perfect nature. God could never will us to do anything evil, because he is goodness itself and desires that we be made holy because he is holy (1 Pet. 1:16). The *Catechism*, quoting St. Thomas Aquinas, teaches that "God's almighty power is in no way arbitrary: 'In God, power, essence, will, intellect, wisdom, and justice are all identical. Nothing therefore can be in God's power which could not be in his just will or his wise intellect'" (CCC 271).

[31] Jennifer Jackson, *Ethics in Medicine: Virtue, Vice, and Medicine* (Cambridge: Polity Press, 2006), 140.

Chapter 6: Why We Believe in Jesus

[32] I owe this insight to the Christian philosopher Randal Rauser.

[33] Josephus, *Antiquities of the Jews*, 18.3.3; see also 20.9.1.

[34] Tacitus, *Annals*, 15.44.

[35] Bart Ehrman, *Did Jesus Exist? The Historical Argument for Jesus of Nazareth* (New York: HarperOne, 2012), 4.

[36] From "The Buddha's Farewell Address" in Paul Carus, *The Gospel of Buddha, Compiled from Ancient Records* (Chicago and London: Open Court Publishing Company, 1915).

[37] This copy is called Codex Sinaiticus because it was discovered in a monastery at the foot of Mount Sinai.

[38] For a defense of the reliability of the Gospels see Craig Blomberg's *The Historical Reliability of the Gospels* (Downers Grove, Ill.: InterVarsity Press, 2007) and *The Historical Reliability of John's Gospel* (Downers Grove, Ill.: InterVarsity Press, 2011).

[39] F.F. Bruce, *The Books and the Parchments: How We Got Our English Bible* (Grand Rapids, Mich.: Fleming H. Revell Co., 1984), 78.

[40] Therese de Lisieux. Story of a Soul: The Autobiography of St. Thérèse of Lisieux, 3rd ed., trans. John Clarke (Washington, D.C.: ICS Publications, 1996), 100-101.

Chapter 7: Why We Believe in the Resurrection

[41] John Dominic Crossan, *Jesus: A Revolutionary Biography* (San Francisco:

HarperCollins, 2009), 163.

[42] Gerd Lüdemann, *What Really Happened to Jesus?*, trans. John Bowden (Louisville, Ky.: Westminster John Knox Press, 1995), 80.

[43] William Edwards, Wesley Gabel, and Floyd Hosmer, "On the Physical Death of Jesus Christ," *Journal of the American Medical Association,* 255, no. 11 (March 21, 1986), 1457.

[44] The skeleton belongs to Yehohanan of the village Giv'at Ha-Mivtar. Matthew W. Maslen and Piers D. Mitchell, "Medical Theories on the Cause of Death in Crucifixion," *Journal of the Royal Society of Medicine* 99, no. 4 (2006), 185-88.

[45] Gary R. Habermas and J.P. Moreland, *Immortality: The Other Side of Death* (Nashville, Tenn.: Nelson, 1992), 60.

[46] Gary R. Habermas and Antony Flew, "My Pilgrimage from Atheism to Theism: An Exclusive Interview with Former British Atheist Professor Antony Flew," Faculty Publications and Presentations of Liberty University Paper, 2004, 333.

[47] Buddha is recorded as saying in Sutta 11.5 of the Digha Nikaya, "Seeing the danger of such miracles, I dislike, reject and despise them." Sura 13:7 of the Qu'ran says, "Those who disbelieved say, 'Why has a sign not been sent down to him from his Lord?' You are only a warner, and for every people is a guide." Muhammad's role was simply to preach about Allah, not perform any miracles.

[48] Gary Habermas and Michael Licona, *The Case for the Resurrection of Jesus* (Grand Rapids, Mich.: Kregel Publications, 2004), 70.

[49] St. Justin Martyr, *Dialogue with Trypho*, chapter CVIII.

[50] Talmud, Sotah 3:4, 19a (cited in Rachel Keren, "Torah Study," in *Jewish Women: A Comprehensive Historical Encyclopedia,* March 20, 2009, Jewish Women's Archive, http://jwa.org/encyclopedia/article/torah-study); and Talmud Rosh Hashanah, 22a.

[51] Josephus, *Antiquities of the Jews*, 4.8.15.

[52] Pope St. Clement, a disciple of St. Peter, wrote in his letter to the Corinthians that Peter, for example, "through unrighteous envy, endured not one or two, but numerous labors, and when he had finally suffered martyrdom, departed to the place of glory due to him. Owing to envy, Paul also obtained the reward of patient endurance . . . and suffered martyrdom under the prefects" (*First Clement*, 5:4-5). St. Polycarp of Smyrna, who was a disciple of St. John, describes Jesus' endurance till death and similarly exhorts believers to "practice all endurance, which also you saw with your own eyes in the blessed Ignatius and Zosimus

and Rufus, and in others also who came from among yourselves, as well as in Paul himself and the rest of the apostles" (*Letter to the Philippians*, 9.1). Because Clement and Polycarp personally knew the apostles, we can have a high degree of confidence in their testimony that St. Peter and St. John were indeed martyred. Finally, Josephus records that James, whom he describes as "the brother of Jesus," was stoned by Caiaphas the high priest for transgressing the law (*Antiquities of the Jews*, 20.9.1).

Chapter 8: Why We Believe in the Trinity

53 Some Mormons claim that the reason they pray only to the Father (whom they call "Heavenly Father") is because Jesus taught his disciples to address their prayers to "our Father" and because Jesus told his disciples to "ask of the Father in my name." Of course, just because Jesus gave us one way to pray does not mean that is the only way to pray. After all, Mormons give thanks to Heavenly Father even though Jesus never showed his followers through the Lord's Prayer how to give thanks to God. It seems more likely that Mormons only pray to the Father because they are following the prescription in the Book of Mormon, where Jesus says, "Ye must always pray unto the Father in my name" (3 Nephi 18:19).

54 Mormons believe that we (along with Jesus) are all God's spirit children. But as one Mormon apologetics website admits, "[I]t is technically true to say that Jesus and Satan are 'brothers,' in the sense that both have the same spiritual parent, God the Father" (en.fairmormon.org/Jesus_Christ/Brother_of_Satan). The belief that we will become Gods is a consequence of the fact that Mormons believe God and man are of the same species. Human beings are simply less developed gods and have the potential to be "exalted," or become gods—provided they follow the teachings of the Church of Latter-day Saints. Joseph Smith said in the King Follett sermon, "Here, then, is eternal life—to know the only wise and true God; and you have got to learn how to be gods yourselves, and to be kings and priests to God, the same as all gods have done before you, namely, by going from one small degree to another, and from a small capacity to a great one; from grace to grace, from exaltation to exaltation." For more, see my booklet *20 Answers: Mormonism*.

55 In Isaiah 44:8 God says, "Is there a God besides me? I know not any." If the God of this world were omniscient, then wouldn't he know about the God that he worshipped when he was a man? God also makes it clear in Isaiah 43:10 that "Before me no god was formed, nor shall there

be any after me." This can't refer to false gods or idols, because many of those are still "formed" to this day. Instead, the Bible teaches that no other God besides the one true God has ever existed, and no other God ever will exist. The New Testament also firmly teaches there is only one God. Jesus described God as "the only God" (John 5:44) and "the only true God" (John 17:3). St. Paul describes God as "the only wise God" (Rom. 16:27) and the only being who possesses immortality (1 Tim. 6:16).

[56] "[T]he scriptures point to the resurrected Jesus Christ as the chief of all angels—Michael the archangel." "Who is Michael the Archangel?" Awake! February 8, 2002, 17, http://wol.jw.org/en/wol/d/r1/lp-e/102002085. However, the Bible teaches that Jesus is not an angel, so this claim is false (Heb. 1:4-6).

[57] The Greek word for "firstborn," *prototokos,* can refer to a special position someone has that is worthy of honor and privilege, and not only to the literal order of birth among siblings. For example, in Psalm 89:27 God says of David, "I will make him the first-born, the highest of the kings of the earth." Obviously, David was not the first king to reign among the kings of the Earth. He was instead placed in a position of preeminence or authority over all other kings. But just as the firstborn of kings is the one who rules over kings, it follows that the firstborn of creation, or Jesus, as Colossians 1:15 describes him, is the one who rules over creation.

[58] When the Bible says, "God raised Jesus from the dead," it refers to the Father, the Son (John 2:19-21), and the Holy Spirit all raising him from the dead. See also CCC 648.

[59] Tertullian, *Against Praxeas,* 2.

Chapter 9: Why We Believe in the Bible

[60] CCC 390.

[61] William G. Dever, *Who Were the Early Israelites and Where Did They Come From?* (Grand Rapids, Mich.: Wm. B. Eerdmans), 202.

[62] Jeffrey H. Schwartz, *What the Bones Tell Us* (New York: Henry Holt, 2015), 29-30.

[63] Karl Keating, *Catholicism and Fundamentalism: The Attack on Romanism by Bible Christians* (San Francisco: Ignatius Press, 1988), 126.

[64] St. Augustine, *Against the Fundamental Epistle of Manichaeus*, 5.

Chapter 10: Why We Aren't Bible-Only Christians

[60] Another verse that is cited in defense of *sola scriptura* is Acts 17:11, which describes how the Jews in Beroea "were more noble than those in Thessalonica, for they received the word with all eagerness, examining the scriptures daily to see if [Paul's teaching was true]." But the Jews in Thessalonica were not ignorant of Scripture. They just opposed Paul's interpretation of Scripture because he "reasoned" and "proved" from it that Jesus was the Messiah. The Beroeans, on the other hand, were more "noble" because they were open-minded and saw that Scripture was a witness to Paul's preaching. Luke even acknowledges that "the word of God was proclaimed by Paul at Beroea" (Acts 17:13), which means that the word of God is not confined to written words alone.

[66] The *Catechism* says, "The Tradition here in question comes from the apostles and hands on what they received from Jesus' teaching and example and what they learned from the Holy Spirit" (CCC 83).

[67] St. Irenaeus, *Against Heresies,* 1:10:2, 3:4:1.

[68] It was also defined in the face of Protestant criticism of the canon at the ecumenical Council of Trent (1545-1563).

[69] Douglas Wilson, "A Severed Branch," *Credenda Agenda* 12, no. 1, www.credenda.org/archive/issues/12-1thema.php.

[70] Eusebius, *Church History,* 4:23:11.

[71] R.C. Sproul, *What Is Reformed Theology? Understanding the Basics* (Grand Rapids, Mich.: Baker Books, 2005), 54.

[72] Consider the group that wants to remove from the Bible the story about Jesus having mercy on the woman caught in adultery (John 7:53-8:11), www.conservapedia.com/Essay:Adulteress_Story.

[73] For a defense of the inspiration of the deuterocanonical books see Gary Michuta, *The Case for the Deuterocanon: Evidence and Arguments* (Livonia, Mich.: Nikaria Press, 2015).

[74] See 2 Maccabees 12:46 for one example.

[75] St. Vincent of Lerins, *Commonitory,* 2.5

Chapter 11: Why We Belong to the Catholic Church

[76] St. Ignatius of Antioch, *Letter to the Smyrnaeans*, 8.

[77] Ibid.

[78] Pope St. Clement, *Letter to the Corinthians,* 44:1-3.

[79] St. Justin Martyr, *First Apology*, 65.

[80] St. Ignatius of Antioch, *Letter to the Trallians,* 2:1.

[81] Tertullian, *Baptism*, 1.

[82] Origen, *Commentaries on Romans* 5:9.
[83] St. Cyprian, *The Lapsed*, 28.
[84] Pope St. John Paul II, *Redemptoris Missio*, 52.
[85] The text describes the servant as a eunuch. A eunuch was a man who had been castrated so that he could be trusted to guard female members of the royal family and not become sexually involved with them. In the ancient world it also referred to men who were impotent or otherwise incapable of engaging in sexual intercourse.
[86] John Calvin, *A Treatise of the Eternal Predestination Of God*, 38.
[87] St. Augustine, *Against the Letter of Mani Called "The Foundation,"* 4:5.

Chapter 12: Why We Have a Pope

[88] J.N.D. Kelly, *The Oxford Dictionary of the Popes* (Oxford: Oxford University Press, 1996), 1.
[89] Didn't Peter refer to himself as a "fellow elder" and not as "pope" in 1 Peter 5:1? Yes, but in this passage Peter is demonstrating humility, which he is encouraging other priests to practice. He wrote, "Clothe yourselves, all of you, with humility toward one another" (5:5), so exalting his status would have contradicted his message. Addressing his audience as "fellow elders" no more invalidates his leadership then when the president addresses the nation as "my fellow Americans." Besides, St. Paul often referred to himself as a mere deacon (1 Cor. 3:5, 2 Cor. 11:23) and even said he was "the very least of all the saints" (Eph. 3:8)—but that did not take away from his authority as an apostle.
[90] Craig Keener, *The Gospel of Matthew: A Socio-Rhetorical Commentary* (Grand Rapids, Mich.: Wm. B. Eerdmans, 2009), 426.
[91] Some people quote Pope Leo X (1513-1521) as saying, "How profitable that fable of Christ has been to us and our company," to show that a medieval pope was the Antichrist because he thought Jesus was a myth created to justify the existence of a power-hungry Church. But the problem with this quote is that while it does come from the sixteenth century, Pope Leo X never said it. This quote actually comes from the Protestant dissenter John Bale's satirical book *The Pageant of Popes,* and was an amateur attempt to smear the Roman pontiff's character.
[92] Jesus speaks of "you all" with the Greek word *hymas* in verse 31, but in the next verse Jesus uses the Greek word *sou*, which is the singular "you" in reference to Peter.
[93] In this situation Peter, at most, made an error in behavior, not teaching. Peter feared antagonism from Christians who thought circumcision

was necessary for salvation. So, while he was in their presence, Peter declined to eat with the uncircumcised. Paul criticized Peter for doing this, but Paul himself accommodated this same group when he had his disciple Timothy circumcised. Paul did this to make it easier to preach to the Jews (Acts 16:1-3), but he called circumcision a grave sin in Galatians 5:2. Therefore, if prudentially yielding to critics doesn't invalidate St. Paul's authority, then neither does it invalidate St. Peter's.

[94] Thomas R. Schreiner, *Galatians* (Grand Rapids, Mich.: Zondervan, 2010), 145.

[95] St. Cyrpian, *Epistle*, 54.14

[96] Eusebius, *Church History*, 4:23:9

[97] St. Irenaeus, *Against Heresies*, 3.3.2

[98] Prosper, Account I, sourcebooks.fordham.edu/source/attila2.asp.

Chapter 13: Why We Have Priests

[99] This account comes from third-class passenger Helen Mary Mocklare and was published in the *New York World* on April 22, 1912.

[100] Joseph Pronechen, "Father Thomas Byles: God's Faithful Servant on the Titanic," *National Catholic Register*, April 15, 2015, www.ncregister.com/daily-news/father-thomas-byles-gods-faithful-servant-on-the-titanic.

[101] St. Cyprian, *The Lapsed*, 28.

[102] The Church does not teach that women are inferior to men and that is why they cannot be priests. God's eternal wisdom is personified as a woman (Prov. 8) and in Galatians 3:28 Paul says that in Christ there is no difference in value between men and women. At the end of his letter to the Romans, St. Paul refers to various women who acted as co-workers with him in the field of evangelization (Rom. 16). The Church even recognizes that the one creature who deserves to be praised more than any other is a woman—Mary, the Mother of God. But this does not contradict the Church's practice of imitating Christ, who only selected men to be apostles even though many women supported his ministry. Some people say Jesus chose only men to be apostles because that was expected in the culture of his time, but Jesus routinely contradicted the cultural sensitivities of his day. Priestesses were common in ancient mystery religions, yet St. Paul firmly taught that women could not have the same leadership positions in the Church as men (1 Cor. 11:35). Men and women are equal in dignity but they are not identical, so it makes sense God would call each to different vocations.

[103] Some argue that 1 Corinthians 9:5 proves that Peter had a wife during Paul's missionary journeys. Karl Keating responds in this way: "The key Greek words in 1 Corinthians 9:5 are '*adelphaen gunaika*.' The first means 'sister,' and the second can be translated as either 'woman' or 'wife.' This means the phrase translates as 'sister woman' or 'sister wife,' with 'sister' indicating not a biological but a spiritual relationship." See Karl Keating, "Did Peter Have a Wife," *Catholic Answers Magazine* 18, no. 5, May 2007, www.catholic.com/magazine/articles/did-peter-have-a-wife.

[104] A. Jones, "The Gospel of Jesus Christ According to St Matthew," in B. Orchard and E. F. Sutcliffe, eds., *A Catholic Commentary on Holy Scripture* (New York: Thomas Nelson, 1953), 885.

Chapter 14: Why We Go to Mass

[105] Earlier in John's Gospel Jesus used a metaphor involving food that his disciples misunderstood. Jesus said he had food to eat, to which the disciples essentially asked, "Who brought Jesus' lunch" (and maybe wondered, "Why didn't they get us anything!"). Jesus corrected them, saying that he was being metaphorical. He explained, "My food is to do the will of him who sent me, and to accomplish his work" (John 4:34). But in John 6, when people began to abandon Jesus over the supposed metaphor of "eating his flesh," Jesus does not say, "Wait, it's just a metaphor!" Instead he reaffirmed the difficulty of his teaching, and his disciples stood by him because they knew there was no one else they could go to who had the words of eternal life (John 6:68).

[106] St. Ignatius, *Letter to the Smyrnaeans*, 7.

[107] J.N.D. Kelly, *Early Christian Doctrines* (New York: Harper Collins, 1978), 440.

[108] Jesus said to take the Eucharist "in remembrance of me" (Luke 22:19), but he did not mean the Eucharist was only a symbolic representation of him. The word translated "in memory" comes from the Greek word *anamnesis*, which means "to offer a memorial sacrifice." It refers to making something present through a sacrifice. In this case, the body of Jesus Christ is made present when the priest presents to the Father the one sacrifice of Christ, our paschal lamb, under the form of bread and wine. See also Stephen K. Ray, *Crossing the Tiber: Evangelical Protestants Discover the Historical Church* (San Francisco: Ignatius Press, 1997), 210.

[109] Mass is called the "holy sacrifice" because "it makes present the one sacrifice of Christ the Savior and includes the Church's offering . . .

it re-presents (makes present) the sacrifice of the cross" (CCC 1330,1336). Even though Christ said on the cross, "It is finished" (John 19:30), this does not mean nothing else needs to be done to secure our salvation. Romans 8:34 says Christ, at this very moment, intercedes for us before the Father. Re-presenting Christ's sacrifice to the Father does not take away from the unique, saving effect of that sacrifice any more than Christ's current intercession for us takes away from what he did on the cross.

[110] *Didache*, 14. Hebrews 13:10 also reveals that Christians "have an altar from which those who serve the tent have no right to eat," which means that Christians have a sacrifice to offer God. Those who "serve the tent" are the Jewish priests in the Temple who were not allowed to receive the sacrifice of the Eucharist, which only Christians could receive.

[111] Peter Kreeft, "What I Learned from a Muslim About Eucharistic Adoration," catholicity.com, April 21, 2011.

[112] St. Tarcisius, Martyr, www.ewtn.com/library/MARY/TARCISI.htm. Taken from Berchmans Bittle, *A Saint a Day According to the Liturgical Calendar of the Church* (Milwaukee: Bruce Publishing Company, 1958).

Chapter 15: Why We Baptize Babies

[113] "For immersion in water, it was clear to him, could not be used for the forgiveness of sins, but as a sanctification of the body, and only if the soul was already thoroughly purified by right actions," Josephus, *Antiquities of the Jews*, 18.5.2.

[114] "By yielding to the tempter, Adam and Eve committed a personal sin, but this sin affected the human nature that they would then transmit in a fallen state. It is a sin that will be transmitted by propagation to all mankind, that is, by the transmission of a human nature deprived of original holiness and justice. And that is why original sin is called 'sin' only in an analogical sense: it is a sin 'contracted' and not 'committed'—a state and not an act" (CCC 404).

[115] *The Didache*, 7.

[116] St. Cyprian, *Letters*, 64.5.

Chapter 16: Why We Believe in Spite of Scandal

[117] Pope St. Paul VI, *Solemni Hac Liturgia*, 19. Cited in CCC 827.

[118] "The Nature and Scope of Sexual Abuse of Minors by Catholic Priests and Deacons in the United States 1950-2002," research study conduct-

ed by John Jay College of Criminal Justice, City University of New York, for the United States Conference of Catholic Bishops, February 2004, www.usccb.org/issues-and-action/child-and-youth-protection/upload/The-Nature-and-Scope-of-Sexual-Abuse-of-Minors-by-Catholic-Priests-and-Deacons-in-the-United-States-1950-2002.pdf.

[119] Electa Draper, "Scandal creates contempt for Catholic clergy" Denver Post, May 25, 2010, http://blogs.denverpost.com/hark/2010/05/25/scandal-creates-contempt-for-catholic-clergy/39/

[120] Pat Wingert, "Priests Commit No More Abuse Than Other Males," *Newsweek*, April 7, 2010, www.newsweek.com/priests-commit-no-more-abuse-other-males-70625.

[121] "Address of Dr. Monica Applewhite to the Irish Bishops," March 10, 2009, www.themediareport.com/wp-content/uploads/2012/11/Applewhite-Ireland-Address-Bishops-2009.pdf.

[122] Elisabetta Povoledo and Laurie Goodstein, "Pope Creates Tribunal for Bishop Negligence in Child Sexual Abuse Cases," June 10, 2015, www.nytimes.com/2015/06/11/world/europe/pope-creates-tribunal-for-bishop-negligence-in-child-sexual-abuse-cases.html?_r=0.

[123] David Gibson. "10 Years After Catholic Sex Abuse Reforms, What's Changed?," *Washington Post,* June 6, 2012, www.washingtonpost.com/national/on-faith/10-years-after-catholic-sex-abuse-reforms-whats-changed/2012/06/06/gJQAQMjOJV_story.html.

[124] Thomas F. Madden, *The New Concise History of the Crusades* (Lanham, Md.: Rowman & Littlefield Publishers, 2005), vii.

[125] Peter Lock, *The Routledge Companion to the Crusades* (New York: Routledge, 2006), 412.

[126] Cited in S.J. Allen and Emilie Amt, eds., *The Crusades: A Reader*, 2nd. ed., (Toronto: University of Toronto Press, 2014), 35.

[127] Thomas E. Woods Jr., "The Myth of Hitler's Pope: An Interview with Rabbi David G. Dalin," Catholic Exchange, July 29, 2005, catholicexchange.com/the-myth-of-hitlers-pope-an-interview-with-rabbi-david-g-dalin.

[128] Julian the Apostate, *Letter to Arsacius*.

[129] Roy Porter, *The Greatest Benefit to Mankind: A Medical History of Humanity* (New York: HarperCollins, 1997), 88.

[130] Anthony Fisher, *Catholic Bioethics for a New Millennium* (Cambridge: Cambridge University Press, 2012), 279-80.

[131] Leprosy is now known as Hansen's disease.

[132] *Butler's Lives of the Saints,* vol. 4, 106.

Chapter 17: Why We Believe in Faith Working Through Love

[133] For a good treatment of this issue see Jimmy Akin, *The Drama of Salvation* (San Diego, Calif.: Catholic Answers Press, 2015), especially chapter 2.

[134] "Despite repeated assurances that AIDS has been shown to be transmitted only through intimate sexual contact or through the exchange of blood, some neighbors remain fearful that the virus could be transmitted through the air. Others disapprove of the fact that the home is caring for gay men." Sandra G. Boodman, "Neighbors Are Fearful of Nuns' Caring for the Dying in Convent," *Washington Post*, January 12, 1987, B01.

[135] Mae Elise Cannon, *Just Spirituality: How Faith Practices Fuel Social Action* (Downers Grove, Ill.: InterVarsity Press, 2013), 19.

Chapter 18: Why We Believe in Purgatory

[136] C.S. Lewis, *Letters to Malcolm: Chiefly on Prayer* (New York: Mariner Books, 2002), 108-109. Although Lewis was critical of some medieval conceptions of purgatory, he affirms the depiction of the sinner in Cardinal Newman's poem "Dream of Gerontius," seeking purification before God's throne.

[137] See also CCC 1855-59.

[138] Pope Benedict XVI, *Spe Salvi*, 47. For a thorough treatment of the good thief on the cross and its relation to purgatory, see Jim Blackburn, "Dismissing the Dismas Case," *Catholic Answers Magazine*, 23, no. 2, March 2012.

[139] Martin Luther, *Defense and Explanations of All the Articles*, Article 37.

[140] In the Middle Ages one of the acts of charity that could be done to obtain an indulgence was to give money to the poor, or alms. Although this is a virtuous and good act, some people only saw it as a transaction and did not give money in a spirit of humble repentance for sin. Therefore, the Church removed almsgiving as a work associated with the granting of indulgences.

[141] *Spe Salvi*, 47.

[142] Some people say praying to saints violates Deuteronomy 18:11, which forbids the sin of necromancy. But that refers to using magic to summon the souls of the dead (like when Saul summoned Samuel's soul from the dead with the help of the witch of Endor in 1 Samuel 28:3-19). It is not always wrong to talk to the dead, since Jesus spoke with Moses on the Mount of Transfiguration and Moses had been dead for centuries (Matt. 17:3).

Chapter 19: Why We Pray to Saints

[143] Paul also says that death does not separate us from the love of Christ (Rom. 8:39), so if we are all united to Christ, then we are united to one another in a bond of faith and love.

[144] William Barclay, *The Letter to the Hebrews* (Louisville, Ky.: Westminster John Knox Press, 1976), 202.

[145] Even if the devil doesn't personally tempt us, and only his demons do, Satan himself is organizing all of this. This means that, in order to lead his demonic kingdom, he has mental abilities that far surpass what humans in this life possess.

[146] St. Clement of Alexandria, *Miscellanies,* 7:12.

[147] Robert Milburn, *Early Christian Art and Architecture* (Oakland, Calif.: University of California Press, 1991), 38.

[148] Elizabeth Vargas and Donna Hunter, "Miracle of Faith: The Work of a Saint?," ABC News, April 2, 2010, abcnews.go.com/2020/miracle-faith-chase-kear-recovers-fatal-accident-prayers/story?id=10239513.

Chapter 20: Why We Honor Mary

[149] When God the Son became man, he remained a divine person with a divine nature. In becoming man, however, he assumed an additional human nature and was conceived in Mary's womb, from which he was born.

[150] Timothy George, "The Blessed Virgin Mary in Evangelical Perspective," *Mary, Mother of God*, eds., Carl E. Braaten and Robert W. Jenson (Grand Rapids, Mich.: Wm. B. Eerdmans, 2004), 110.

[151] See *Luther's Commentary on The Magnificat*. Cited in Beth Kreitzer, *Reforming Mary: Changing Images of the Virgin Mary in Lutheran Sermons of the Sixteenth Century* (New York: Oxford University Press, 2004) 53.

[152] John Calvin, *Commentary on a Harmony of the Evangelists Matthew, Mark, and Luke*, section 39.

[153] This word is used to describe Abram and his nephew Lot (Gen. 14:14) as well as the cousins of Moses and Aaron (Lev. 10:4).

[154] "According to Scripture and ancient Jewish tradition, Mary belonged to the father of her child—the Holy Spirit. However, the Holy Spirit could not be the protector that Mary needed. The Holy Spirit could not sign legal documents and be Mary's legal spouse. But Joseph was ready and willing—just man that he was—to care for Mary as his lawfully wedded spouse." Tim Staples, *Behold Your Mother: A Biblical and*

Historical Defense of the Marian Doctrines (San Diego, Calif.: Catholic Answers Press, 2014), 247.

[155] Ibid. 83-103.

[156] St. Irenaeus, *Against Heresies,* 3:22:24.

Chapter 21: Why We Protect Life

[157] *Didache*, 2.

[158] Pope Benedict XVI, *Deus Caritas Est*, 28.

[159] Pope St. John Paul II, *Evangelium Vitae,* 99.

[160] Ronan R. O'Rahilly and Fabiola Müller, *Human Embryology & Teratology*, third edition. (New York: Wiley-Liss, 2001), 8. The full quote reads: "Although human life is a continuous process, fertilization (which, incidentally, is not a 'moment') is a critical landmark because, under ordinary circumstances, a new, genetically distinct human organism is formed when the chromosomes of the male and female pronuclei blend in the oocyte."

[161] Some people understand why abortion is wrong, but still think assisted suicide is okay. They say, "The baby never had a choice, but shouldn't someone in terrible pain be allowed to die if that's what he wants?" Catholics believe everyone deserves to be treated with dignity and have access to treatment for pain. It's even okay to give a dying person pain medication that, as an unintended side effect, speeds up the natural process of dying. But we rob sick people of their dignity when we say that healthy people deserve to be talked out of suicide because they have "lives worth living," but the sick or disabled are better off ending their own lives. By making it legal to help someone end his life, this pressures other sick and disabled people, who may feel like they are a burden on their loved ones, to do the same thing. We euthanize sick and unwanted pets because even though we don't want them to suffer we don't believe it is appropriate to treat their suffering with expensive medicine or round-the-clock human care. But shouldn't *humans* receive appropriate levels of human care? That is why the Church encourages doctors to kill disease or kill pain, but not to kill their own patients.

[162] Richard Stith, "Arguing with Pro-Choicers," *First Things*, November 4, 2006, www.firstthings.com/onthesquare/2006/11/stith-arguing-with-pro-choicer.

[163] In Stith's original essay he uses the example of a jaguar that has leaped back into dense jungle foliage. My friend and fellow pro-life colleague

Stephanie Gray combines Stith's argument with the example of the Loch Ness monster.

[164] Bernard Nathanson, *The Hand of God* (Washington, D.C.: Regnery Publishing, 1996), 58-60. Nathanson admits that at the time, "I had no feelings aside from the sense of accomplishment, the pride of expertise."

[165] Bernard Nathanson, *Aborting America* (Pinnacle Books, 1981), 193.

[166] Nathanson, *The Hand of God,* 202.

Chapter 22: Why We Cherish Our Sexuality

[167] Juve Shiver, Jr., "Television Awash in Sex, Study Says," *Los Angeles Times,* November 10, 2005.

[168] Karol Wojtyla, *Love and Responsibility* (San Francisco: Ignatius Press, 1993), 272.

[169] For this particular argument I am indebted to the writings of Karol Wojtyla, Christopher West, Janet Smith, and Alex Pruss.

[170] Marcus Aurelius, *Meditations*, 6:13.

[171] Peter Singer, *Practical Ethics* (New York: Cambridge University Press, 2011), 2.

[172] This example comes from Sherif Gergis, Robert George, and Ryan Anderson, *What Is Marriage? Man and Woman: A Defense* (New York: Encounter Books, 2012), 25.

[173] Daniel T. Lichter, Katherine Michelmore, Richard N. Turner, and Sharon Sassler, "Pathways to a Stable Union? Pregnancy and Childbearing Among Cohabiting and Married Couples," *Population Research and Policy Review*, 35, no. 3 (June 2016), 377-99.

Chapter 23: Why We Defend Marriage

[174] *Code of Canon Law*, 1055.

[175] Wendy Wang and Kim Parker, "Record Share of Americans Have Never Married," Pew Research Center, September, 24, 2014, www.pewsocialtrends.org/2014/09/24/record-share-of-americans-have-never-married/.

[176] "In 1963, as President Lyndon Johnson was launching the War on Poverty, 7 percent of American children were born outside marriage ... According to CDC, a record 40.6 percent of children born in 2008 were born outside marriage—a total of 1.72 million children." Robert Rector, "National Review: Out Of Wedlock," NPR, April 12, 2010, www.npr.org/templates/story/story.php?storyId=125848718. "The

percentage of all births to unmarried women was 40.2% in 2014, down from 40.6% in 2013, the lowest level since 2007. This percentage peaked in 2009 at 41.0%. In 2014, the percentage of nonmarital births varied widely among population groups, from 16.4% for [Asian Pacific Islander] mothers to 70.9% for non-Hispanic black mothers." Hamilton, et al. "Births: Final Data for 2014" National Vital Statistics Reports Volume 64, Number 12, December 23, 2015, https://www.cdc.gov/nchs/data/nvsr/nvsr64/nvsr64_12.pdf.

177 Rose M. Kreider and Renee Ellis, "Living Arrangements of Children: 2009," United States Census Bureau, June 2011, https://www.census.gov/prod/2011pubs/p70-126.pdf.

178 D. L. Blackwell, "Family Structure and Children's Health in the United States: Findings from the National Health Interview Survey, 2001-2007," National Center for Health Statistics, *Vital Health Statistics* 10 (2010), 246. Cited in *Family Structure,* December 2015, www.childtrends.org/wp-content/uploads/2015/03/59_Family_Structure.pdf.

179 W. Bradford Wilcox, "Suffer the Little Children: Cohabitation and the Abuse of America's Children," *Public Discourse,* April 22, 2011, www.thepublicdiscourse.com/2011/04/3181/.

180 In the parallel passage in Matthew 19:9, Jesus says, "whoever divorces his wife, except for unchastity, and marries another, commits adultery." Scholars debate the meaning of "unchastity," but it probably refers to adultery that takes place after the betrothal period but before the consummation of the marriage, or it may refer to sexually unlawful marriages that involve close relatives.

181 According to the *Catechism*, "Between the baptized, 'a ratified and consummated marriage cannot be dissolved by any human power or for any reason other than death.' The separation of spouses while maintaining the marriage bond can be legitimate in certain cases provided for by canon law. If civil divorce remains the only possible way of ensuring certain legal rights, the care of the children, or the protection of inheritance, it can be tolerated and does not constitute a moral offense." The *Catechism* goes on to affirm, though, that "Divorce is a grave offense against the natural law. It claims to break the contract, to which the spouses freely consented, to live with each other till death" (CCC 2382-84).

182 The full text says, "Then Judah said to Onan, 'Go in to your brother's wife, and perform the duty of a brother-in-law to her, and raise up off-

spring for your brother.' But Onan knew that the offspring would not be his; so when he went in to his brother's wife he spilled the semen on the ground, lest he should give offspring to his brother. And what he did was displeasing in the sight of the Lord, and he slew him also (Gen. 38:8-10). Normally in the Old Testament the punishment for not raising up children for a deceased brother (or practicing Levirate marriage) was public shaming (Deut. 25:5-10). The fact that the Lord slew Onan is evidence that he was displeased with the way Onan disobeyed his law, that is, by practicing contraception.

[183] "Known and Probable Human Carcinogens," *American Cancer Society,* November 3, 2016, www.cancer.org/cancer/cancercauses/othercarcinogens/generalinformationaboutcarcinogens/known-and-probable-human-carcinogens.

[184] M. A. Wilson, "The Practice of Natural Family Planning Versus the Use of Artificial Birth Control: Family, Moral and Sexual Issues," *Catholic Social Science Review*, 7 (2005), 185-211.

[185] "Holy Mass and Canonization of the Blesseds: Vincenzo Grossi, Mary of the Immaculate Conception, Ludovico Martin and Maria Azelia Guérin," Homily of His Holiness Pope Francis, October 18, 2005, w2.vatican.va/content/francesco/en/homilies/2015/documents/papa-francesco_20151018_omelia-canonizzazioni.html.

[186] Ferdinand Holböck, *Married Saints and Blesseds: Through the Centuries* (San Francisco: Ignatius Press, 2002), 411.

Chapter 24: Why We Believe in Hell

[187] Caryle Murphy, "Most Americans Believe in Heaven . . . and Hell," Pew Research Center, November 10, 2015, www.pewresearch.org/fact-tank/2015/11/10/most-americans-believe-in-heaven-and-hell/.

[188] In the Old Testament the word "hell" usually referred to *sheol*, or the abode of the dead. The Church teaches that after his Crucifixion, Christ preached to the spirits in *sheol* (1 Pet. 4:6), an event the Apostles' Creed refers to as Christ's "descent into hell." Regarding this event, the *Catechism* clearly says, "Jesus did not descend into hell to deliver the damned, nor to destroy the hell of damnation, but to free the just who had gone before him" (CCC 633).

[189] Gehenna was in the valley of Hinnom, which 2 Kings 23:10 and Jeremiah 7:31-32 refer to as a site of child sacrifice.

[190] Pope St. John Paul II, General Audience, July 28, 1999.

[191] In contrast to the traditional view of hell, "annihilationists" say hell is

temporary and God will eventually destroy the damned. They claim the Greek word rendered "eternal" in this passage, *aionios*, means "age" or "a long period of time" and doesn't necessarily mean "forever." But Matthew always uses this word to mean "eternal." Also, in this context Jesus is making a comparison between the eternal life the righteous will enjoy forever and the eternal punishment the wicked will endure forever. The comparison doesn't make sense if the wicked are destroyed and don't have an everlasting existence like the righteous will. Others argue that the Greek word rendered "punishment," *kolasin*, is derived from a word that means to "prune" or "cut off." Therefore, hell is just separation from God by being annihilated or destroyed. It is not eternal, conscious punishment. But analyzing a word's meaning from its etymology can lead to gross errors. After all, the word "virtue" is derived from the Latin word *vir*, which means "man," but that doesn't mean all virtuous people are "manly" people. As any Greek dictionary will tell you, *kolasin* just means "punishment" and *kolasin aionion* means "eternal" or "everlasting punishment."

[192] Tertullian, *A Treatise on the Soul,* 31.

[193] St. Irenaeus, *Against Heresies*, II.33.1.

[194] Pope Benedict XVI, *Spe Salvi*, 45.

Chapter 25: Why We Believe in Heaven

[195] Harold Myra and Marshall Shelley, *The Leadership Secrets of Billy Graham* (Grand Rapids, Mich.: Zondervan, 2005), 49.

[196] Pope John Paul II, General Audience, July 28, 1999.

[197] Pope Paul VI, *Lumen Gentium*, 16. This paragraph also says, "nor does divine providence deny the helps necessary for salvation to those who, without blame on their part, have not yet arrived at an explicit knowledge of God and with his grace strive to live a good life. Whatever good or truth is found amongst them is looked upon by the Church as a preparation for the Gospel. She knows that it is given by Him who enlightens all men so that they may finally have life. But often men, deceived by the Evil One, have become vain in their reasonings and have exchanged the truth of God for a lie, serving the creature rather than the Creator."

About the Author

TRENT HORN is a staff apologist for Catholic Answers who specializes in teaching Catholics to graciously and persuasively engage those who disagree with them. Trent has a master's degree in theology from Franciscan University of Steubenville and is currently pursuing a graduate degree in philosophy from Holy Apostles College. He is the author of three books: *Answering Atheism*, *Persuasive Pro-life*, and *Hard Sayings: A Catholic Approach to Answering Bible Difficulties*.